◇ WINTER ◇
ACTIVITIES

SEASONAL PROJECTS
FOR KIDS   PRE K - 3

Written by Denise Bieniek
Illustrated by Dana Regan

Troll Associates

Metric Conversion Chart

1 inch = 2.54 cm
1 foot = .305 m
1 yard = .914 m
1 mile = 1.61 km
1 fluid ounce = 29.573 ml
1 dry ounce = 28.35 g
1 pound = 0.45 kg
1 cup = .24 l
1 pint = .473 l
1 teaspoon = 4.93 ml

Conversion from Fahrenheit to Celsius: subtract 32 and then multiply the remainder by $\frac{5}{9}$.

ISBN: 0-8167-3189-6

Printed in the United States of America.

10 9 8 7 6 5 4 3 2 1

Contents

INTRODUCTION

Dear Teachers,

By the time winter rolls around, things have settled down in the classroom. Students are familiar with the routines, the room is in pretty good shape, the first report cards and parent-teacher conferences are done, and you can breathe a sigh of relief.

But the holiday season has begun, and your students won't be able to keep from talking and thinking about all the excitement coming up. A teacher's job often gets ten times harder just to keep the class focused on their work.

The projects in this book provide you with many opportunities to involve your students in winter-related activities. Students will enjoy learning about winter celebrations around the world as they make crafts, participate in storytelling activities, and learn holiday phrases and customs of other countries. The activities can be shared by groups to instill togetherness among your students, or children can complete the activities individually, gaining self-confidence with each accomplishment.

I learned a long time ago that it helps to encourage children to express their feelings at this time of the year. I incorporate their priorities into my plans. That way we all get satisfaction from our day together. For example, after the first snow, we might discuss how we feel when we see the snow and touch it. We might create our own snowflakes, or carry out experiments about snow. We can read books and poems about snow, and we can make a recipe such as snow cones. In this way, the children are able to express themselves while building skills in a number of different areas.

I hope the activities and suggestions in this book provide you with ideas that will help you and your class enjoy the winter holiday season in many new and exciting ways.

Happy Holidays!

Denise Bieniek, M.S.

It's Snowing!

In many parts of the world, wintertime means cold and snow. If it does snow in your area, try to take the class out during a light snow storm and collect snowflakes on black paper. The shapes are interesting to look at under a microscope or a magnifying glass. Point out to students that each snowflake is different from the others.

If your area is too warm for a snowfall, your class may still enjoy the winter weather by following these instructions on how to make snowflakes.

Materials:
◆ construction paper
◆ scissors
◆ tape
◆ thread

Directions:

1. Distribute a 6" square- or circle-shaped piece of construction paper and scissors to each child. Demonstrate how to fold the shape in half. Then repeat, folding the shape in half again.

2. Show the children the corner of the folded shape that contains all the folds. Cautioning students not to cut that area, have them cut shapes from along the sides of the paper, keeping the paper folded.

3. When the children have made enough cuts, have them open their papers gently to see what their snowflakes look like.

4. Tape one end of a piece of thread to the top of each snowflake and the other end to the lights or ceiling. If there are enough snowflakes, the room will resemble the outdoors on a snowy day.

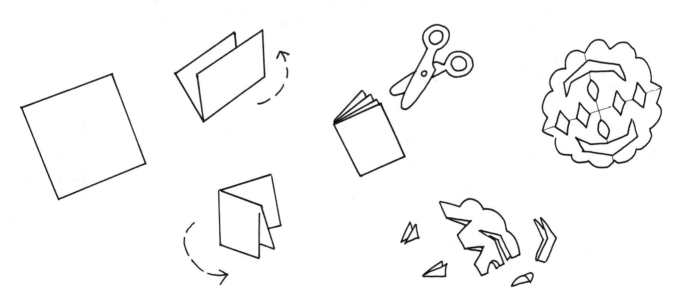

Winter Doorknob Decorations

  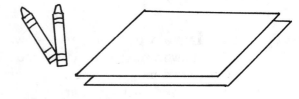

Materials:
- ◆ glue
- ◆ oaktag
- ◆ scissors
- ◆ crayons or markers

Directions:

1. Reproduce the doorknob decorations once for each child.
2. Have children glue the decorations onto oaktag and cut out.
3. Let children color and decorate their work.
4. Cut a slit on the left side of the doorknob holder, then cut out the center circle, as shown.
5. Children may take their doorknob decorations home to use in their bedrooms or playrooms.

Winter Around the World

Tell students that it takes the Earth 365 1/4 days to orbit around the sun. During that time, different parts of the Earth are at varying distances from the sun since the Earth is tipped at an angle. As it revolves around the sun, the Earth's Northern Hemisphere and Southern Hemisphere receive different levels of light and heat. If the Northern Hemisphere is tipped toward the sun, it receives more sun than the Southern Hemisphere and vice versa. If possible, use a globe and a round object to represent the sun to demonstrate this fact.

Explain to the class that countries that lie in the Northern Hemisphere enjoy the arrival of summer while countries in the Southern Hemisphere are gearing up for winter. Six months later, the opposite happens: summer occurs in the Southern Hemisphere and winter in the Northern Hemisphere.

The seasons experienced around the world vary in other ways as well. Countries that are close to the equator would not have snowy winters but countries farther away (and closer to the North or South Pole) have harsher winters. Even within countries, one part of the country may have a cold and snowy winter while the part closer to the equator may have warm weather throughout the winter. For example, in the United States children in Maine may be making snowpeople and going sledding while children in Florida are swimming in the ocean.

Use graphing activities to show what goes on during the winter months. Discuss the weather in your area during a typical winter. What is the average temperature? Graph the temperature for a month and see which temperature occurs the most frequently. What sorts of activities did students do after school and on weekends? Graph them and see which is the most popular. What sorts of clothes have the children been wearing during the winter? Encourage children to identify the types of clothes they have on, specifying the textures, thickness, and number of layers. Do children eat and drink more hot or cold foods in the winter? Ask children to make a chart listing which foods they have eaten for a week or month.

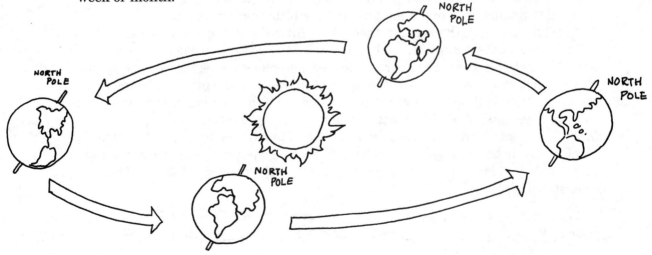

Winter Experiments

Materials:

- ◆ large tub
- ◆ strainers, cups and containers, squeeze bottles, spoons, tubing, funnels
- ◆ clear plastic cups
- ◆ permanent marker
- ◆ string, ounce scale, ruler, measuring tape
- ◆ pot and hot plate

Directions:

1. Provide children with a large tub of water and objects with which they may explore the properties of water, such as strainers, cups and containers of various sizes, squeeze bottles, spoons, tubing, and funnels. Allow several children at a time to experiment with the water until all have had a turn.

2. Discuss what the children learned at the water tub. Write their observations on experience chart paper. Explain that the water they have been touching is called a "liquid."

3. Ask if anyone knows what other forms water may take. Introduce the terms "solid" and "gas." Ask students to think of ways they have seen water as a solid or a gas. Discuss their comments.

4. Help the class see the differences in these forms by performing the following experiments. First, distribute a cup to each child and have him or her fill it halfway with water. Demonstrate how to hold the cup steady on the table while drawing a line on it to mark the water line. Have each child measure how high the water in the cup is by using a ruler or a string. Ask children to record the heights on paper.

5. Let each child put the cup with water on a scale. Note the weight. Then have each child weigh an empty cup alone, and subtract this weight from the water and cup weight to find out the weight of the water. Write the weights on the same paper by each child's name.

6. Inform the class that one way to turn a liquid into a solid is by freezing it. Ask children to predict what might happen once the water has frozen.

7. Let children freeze the water in their cups. After the water has frozen solid, have children look at the water lines. What happened? (The ice is above the lines.)

8. Help children squeeze the ice from the cups and measure the height once again. Have each student write the height of the frozen water on the paper as before and compare. Then help students weigh the ice and see if the weights are different from the liquid weights. Write these weights on the paper as well and compare.

9. To form a gas, heat some water in a pot on a hot plate, making sure that children stand a safe distance away. Ask students to observe what happens once the water starts boiling. Finally, discuss the properties of gas as opposed to the liquid and solid states of water.

Name _____

Helping Children

The United Nations Children's Fund was created on December 12, 1946. The original name of the organization was the United Nations International Children's Emergency Fund, which is why it is called UNICEF. Its first task was to provide food, clothing, and medicine to children who had suffered through World War II.

The UNICEF organization helps children in more than a hundred countries. It provides children with food, medical care, and schooling. UNICEF also helps train people to work as teachers, nurses, and in other important professions. In 1965, the Nobel Peace Prize was awarded to UNICEF.

Find the words associated with UNICEF that are hidden in this puzzle. The words may be written forward, backward, up, down, or diagonally.

G	S	H	E	L	T	E	R	F	E
N	F	E	C	I	N	U	O	F	N
I	B	A	L	A	P	O	G	A	I
H	W	L	M	L	D	N	O	H	C
T	S	T	E	O	U	K	D	T	I
O	C	H	I	L	D	R	E	N	D
L	N	O	I	T	A	C	U	D	E
C	T	R	A	I	N	I	N	G	M

CHILDREN	HELP
CLOTHING	MEDICINE
EDUCATION	SHELTER
FOOD	TRAINING
HEALTH	UNICEF

Don't Catch Cold!

Materials:

- 6 chicken bouillon cubes
- 1 pound boneless, skinless chicken
- 3 carrots
- 3 celery stalks
- 3 scallions
- bag of tortellini or egg noodles
- salt and pepper
- baking pan
- large pot, hot plate
- plastic knives, spoons, bowls or cups

Directions:

1. Place the chicken in a pan and cook at 350°F for 50 minutes. In the large pot, dissolve bouillon cubes in 12 cups of boiling water.

2. Help students cut the carrots, celery, and scallions into small pieces. Add the vegetables to the broth with a pinch of salt and pepper.

3. When the chicken is done, ask several children to cut it into small cubes. Add the chicken to the broth, stirring occasionally.

4. Place the noodles into the mixture and boil for 10 minutes.

5. Using a ladle or a measuring cup, scoop a half cup into each bowl or cup. Distribute the soup with spoons to students. Caution the children that the soup will be hot. This recipe will make about 24 half cups.

What Happened to the Leaves?

Materials:
- ◆ construction paper
- ◆ scissors
- ◆ glue
- ◆ crayons or markers

Directions:
1. Take the class on a walk around the school and look at the trees in the area. Help children remember how full the trees were in autumn compared to how they look now.
2. Discuss the color of any remaining leaves on the trees or on the ground. Encourage students to touch the barks of the trees to see if they too have changed. Ask the children if they know what the trees will look like in the spring and summer.
3. Back in the classroom, show pictures of trees during warmer weather. Compare and contrast these trees with the winter trees. Explain how trees try to conserve water in the fall and winter when water is scarcer. They drop their leaves so there will be less need for water to nourish them. In the spring, when water is more plentiful, the leaves grow back and provide us with shade and beauty.
4. Distribute construction paper, scissors, and glue to the class. Divide students into four groups. Assign each group to one of the four seasons: Fall, Winter, Spring, and Summer.
5. Ask each group to make the base of a tree, including branches. Then ask each group to make their tree resemble a tree from the appropriate season.
6. Cover a bulletin board with sky blue paper and divide it into four sections. Attach each group's tree into one of the sections in order from spring to winter. Then title the trees according to season.
7. On each tree trunk, have children write adjectives that describe that season. Children may write on any season's tree. Title the board, "What Happened to the Leaves?"

WHAT HAPPENED TO THE LEAVES?

SPRING SUMMER FALL WINTER

WINDY WARM COLORFUL COLD

Winter Bird Feeder

Materials:
- ◆ small logs or pine cones
- ◆ empty, clean, half-gallon containers
- ◆ peanut butter
- ◆ paper plates
- ◆ birdseed
- ◆ scissors
- ◆ hole puncher
- ◆ twine

Directions:
1. Ask each child to bring in a small log (approximately 3" in diameter and 5" in length) or a pine cone, and an empty, clean half-gallon container.

2. Spread peanut butter out on several paper plates. Spread birdseed out on several different plates.

3. Have students hold onto the ends of their logs and pine cones and roll them in peanut butter until they are completely covered.

4. Then tell the children to roll the peanut-butter covered logs and pine cones in the birdseed until the objects are covered with the seeds.

5. Show each child how to cut open one side of the container to make room for the log or pine cone.

6. Place the log or pine cone inside the container, as shown. Then punch a hole at the top of the container.

7. Have each student thread sturdy twine through the hole and tie together. Let students take their bird feeders home to hang from trees in their yards, or place the bird feeders in trees on school grounds.

Indoor Basketball Game

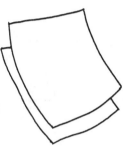

1. Divide the class into groups of four to six children each.
2. Cut the bottom out of a grocery bag, as shown, to make a "basket." Make one basket for each group.
3. Tape the bags along a classroom wall. Leave at least 4' between each basket.
4. Tell each group to form a line in front of their basket. Have the first child in line stand about 3' away from the basket.
5. Crumple up several sheets of butcher paper to make basketballs. Give one ball to each line leader.
6. Tell students to try to shoot the balls into the baskets. After the first child in each line has taken a shot, that child should give the ball to the next child and then go to the end of the line.
7. Let each line keep track of how many baskets it scores. Have each group repeat through their line a designated number of times. Then see which group made the most baskets.
8. As students become more proficient at making baskets, move them back another foot from the basket.

Name _____

You Shoot! You Score!

Add up the numbers on each hockey puck and score a goal for your team. Have a friend help you check your answers. Then add all the sums together on the line at the bottom of the page to find out the number of goals you scored!

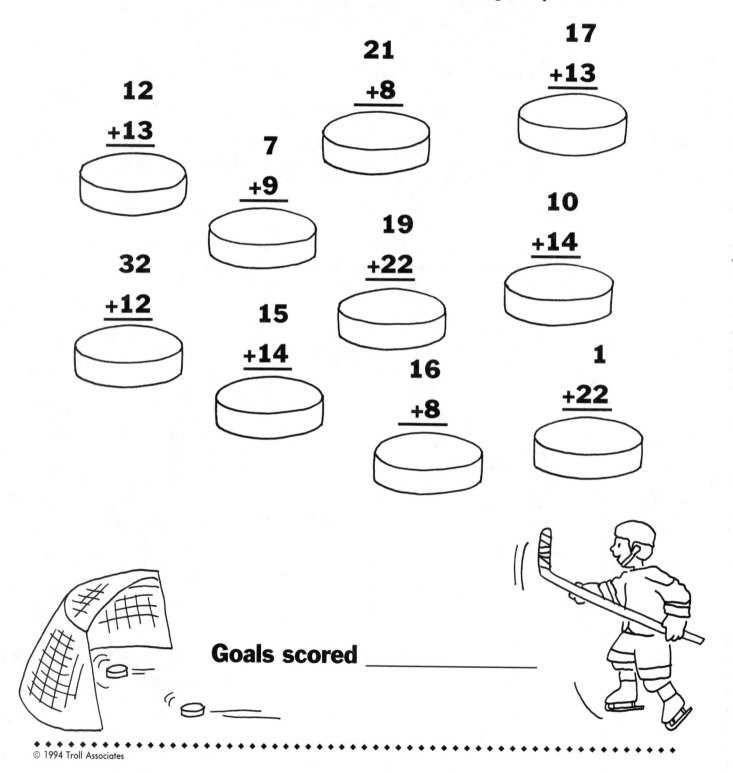

12
+13

21
+8

17
+13

7
+9

32
+12

19
+22

10
+14

15
+14

16
+8

1
+22

Goals scored _____

Human Rights Bulletin Board

1. On December 10, 1948, the United Nations announced its Universal Declaration of Human Rights. This declaration defined the rights of all humans regardless of the country in which they live. It has helped some countries shape their policies on the rights of women and children, as well as the rights of workers.

2. Some of the rights to which all humans are entitled are:

- ◆ the right to life, liberty, and security
- ◆ the right to an education
- ◆ the right to worship as a person wishes
- ◆ the right to live where a person chooses
- ◆ the right to marry and raise a family

3. Discuss with students what might happen, and indeed does happen in some countries, if these goals are not heeded. Have them write and draw their impressions of the declaration on 12" x 18" construction paper.

4. Cover a bulletin board with newspaper. Attach the children's work onto the board and title it "You've Got the Right – So Use It!"

5. When it is time to change the bulletin board, collect the children's work and staple it together to make a class book. Ask several volunteers to design a cover for the book. Leave the book in the reading center for children to enjoy during free time.

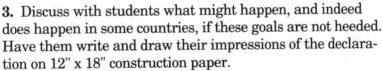

A Trip Around the World

Tell the class that Sir Francis Drake began his trip around the world with five ships and approximately 160 crew members on December 13, 1577. He became the first Englishman to sail around the world, completing the journey on September 26, 1580.

Ask students to imagine what it might be like to sail on a boat seeing new sights and people, eating new foods, surviving fierce storms at sea, getting along with the other people on the ship, and being away from your loved ones for a long time.

Reproduce the map on page 21 once for each child. Then trace with the class the route taken by Sir Francis Drake and his men.

> Drake and his crew began their journey in Plymouth, England. They sailed to Portugal, where they rested and loaded supplies. After Portugal, they headed past the Cape Verde Islands and southwest to the Atlantic Ocean.
> After passing over the equator, they sailed along the South American coast, still heading southwest. It was difficult traveling through the Strait of Magellan, but they succeeded and went on to the port near Santiago, Chile.
> After Chile, Drake planned to go northwest up the coasts of Chile and Peru, then to Panama and the Isthmus. However, fierce storms attacked the ship for over a month and pushed them south. It was then that Drake discovered that there was no land west of the Strait of Magellan as was commonly thought; there was only a vast expanse of ocean.
> Drake and his crew continued northeast back toward Chile, where they rested and repaired their ship. After a time they headed back north toward the Isthmus, passing Lima, Peru, and then traveled north along what is now California.
> Drake then decided to try the "Northwest Passage," which was supposed to connect the Pacific and Atlantic Oceans in the north. However, they could not find the passage, and they realized they had gone too far north when the ship began icing up and the sails stiffened from the cold.
> Defeated, they turned back and sailed west across the Pacific Ocean. The ship stopped at Java, then sailed across the Indian Ocean and around the Cape of Good Hope before heading back to Plymouth, England.

After tracing the voyage, ask the class to guess how far a distance it was from one location to the next. Then have students create a different way of traveling around the world in a ship and have them share their journeys with the class. Encourage the children to use terms such as North, South, East, and West in their discussions.

Name ________________________________

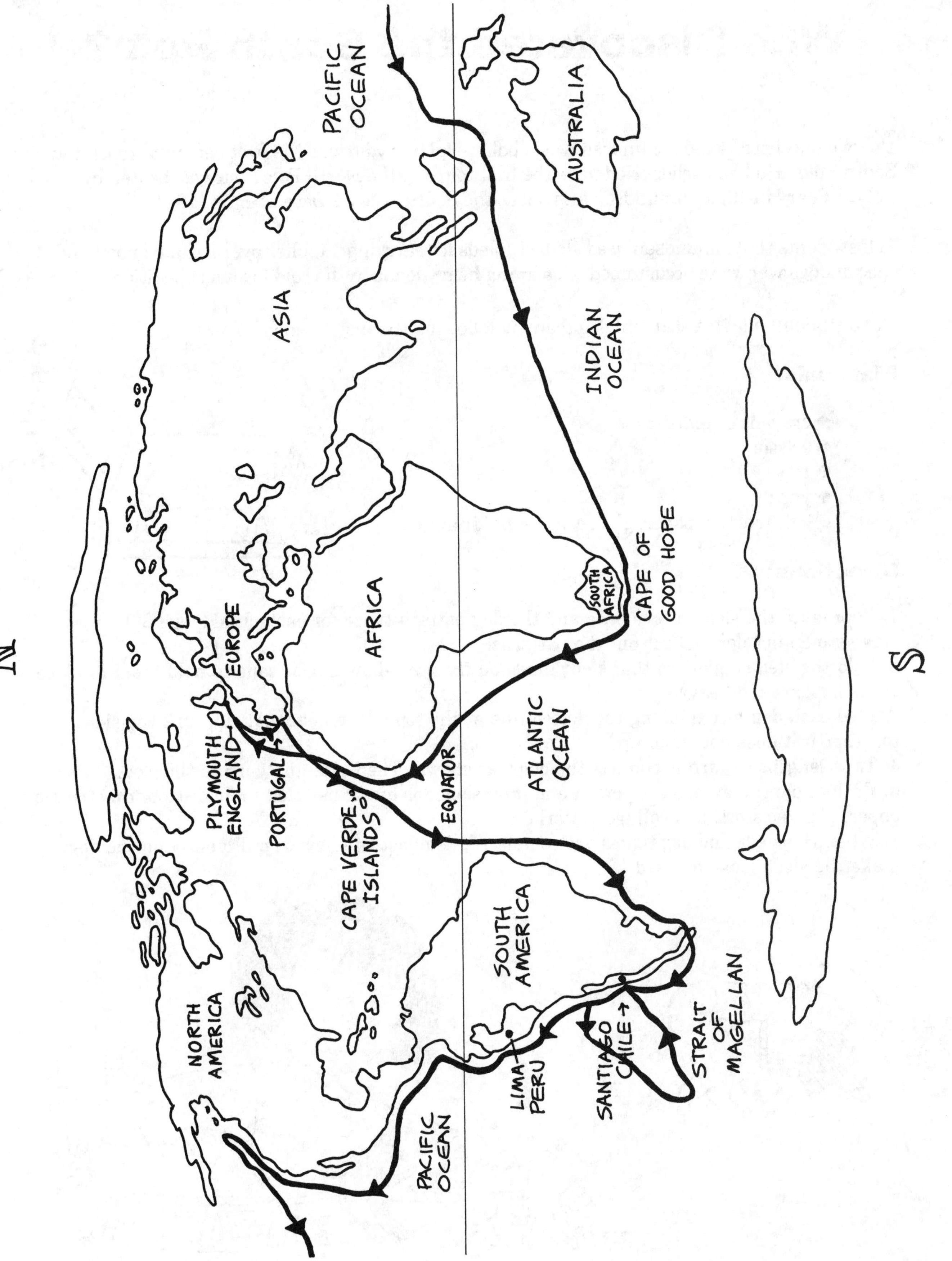
N
S
PACIFIC OCEAN
AUSTRALIA
ASIA
INDIAN OCEAN
AFRICA
SOUTH AFRICA
CAPE OF GOOD HOPE
EUROPE
PLYMOUTH ENGLAND
PORTUGAL
CAPE VERDE ISLANDS
EQUATOR
ATLANTIC OCEAN
NORTH AMERICA
SOUTH AMERICA
LIMA PERU
SANTIAGO CHILE
STRAIT OF MAGELLAN
PACIFIC OCEAN

Who Discovered the South Pole?

Norwegian-born Roald Amundsen was a polar explorer who was the first person to reach the South Pole. He had earlier tried to be the first to reach the North Pole, but was beaten by Robert Peary in 1909. Amundsen arrived at the South Pole on December 14, 1911.

Tell students that Amundsen used sledges (sleds for carrying supplies over ice and snow) and special dogs who were accustomed to carrying heavy loads in the cold for his expedition.

Have students make a sled and dog team by following the instructions below.

Materials:

- ◆ crayons or markers
- ◆ scissors
- ◆ tape
- ◆ yarn
- ◆ construction paper, glue, collage materials

Directions:

1. Reproduce the sled pattern once and the dog pattern twice for each child (page 23). Have students color and cut out the patterns.
2. Fold the sled runners so that sled stands on them as shown. (Use tape to hold them in place if the paper is too heavy.)
3. Fold each dog in half along the dotted line at the top of the head. (Again, tape the sides together if it does not stand up.)
4. Tape lengths of yarn to connect the dogs, as shown. Then tape the yarn to the sled.
5. Each student may make a person and provisions for his or her sled to hold using construction paper, glue, scissors, and collage materials.
6. When the sleds and dog teams are completed, demonstrate how to pull gently on the dogs to make the sleds move forward.

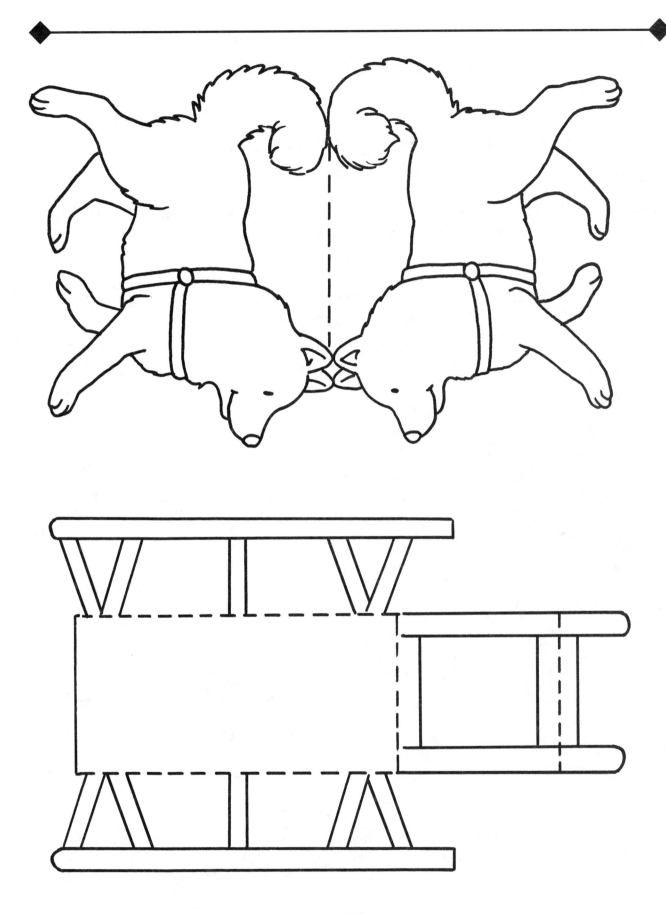

Going My Way?

You are a polar explorer organizing your expedition to the South Pole. You have made up a list of things you want to take.

Cross out the items in the list below you don't think are necessary for the trip. Then tell why you crossed out those items.

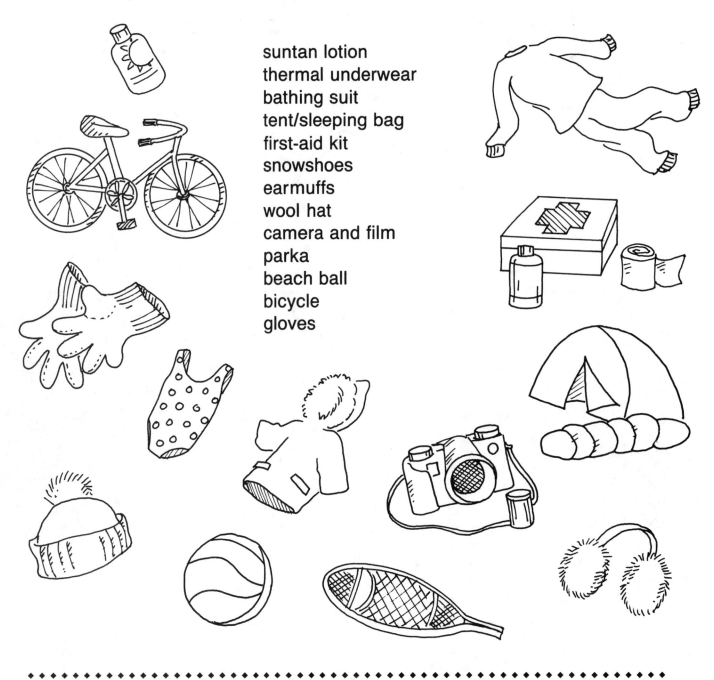

suntan lotion
thermal underwear
bathing suit
tent/sleeping bag
first-aid kit
snowshoes
earmuffs
wool hat
camera and film
parka
beach ball
bicycle
gloves

Penguin Paper-Bag Puppet

Materials:
- crayons or markers
- scissors
- paper lunch bags
- glue
- collage materials

Directions:
1. Reproduce the penguin patterns on page 26 once for each child. Ask students to color the patterns and cut them out.

2. Show the children how to glue the penguin's head to the bottom of a paper lunch bag, facing the crease.

3. Next, have each child glue the body to the large side of the bag, under the penguin's head. Glue the flipper to the body, as shown.

4. Children may wish to add details such as buttons for eyes or noses, and aluminum-foil "fish" to be held in the flippers.

5. Ask children make up short poems about their penguins.

Penguins love the Arctic ice.
They think fish taste very nice.

Penguins like to spend their days
Swimming in a freezing bay.

Penguins waddle when they walk.
They sound funny when they talk.

The Boston Tea Party Flannel Board

In November, 1773, three ships were headed to America from Great Britain. They were carrying crates of tea for the colonists.

But the colonists did not want this tea. The British Parliament had placed a tremendous duty, or tax, on tea exported to the colonies. The price of tea was then cut so the British East India Company could buy all the tea, creating a monopoly that threatened to put colonial merchants out of business. The colonists did not think this tax was fair because they had no representation in the British government, and they protested "taxation without representation."

The ships landed in Boston Harbor at the end of November. The colonists asked the Tea Agents on the ships to head back to Great Britain with the tea. The Tea Agents said that they could not do this unless they received instructions from Great Britain. One of the ship owners tried to get permission to leave, but it was denied.

The colonists met many times to try to decide what to do. If they let the ships unload the tea, it would be the end of many colonists' businesses. If they got rid of the tea, Great Britain would hold the people of Boston responsible. These actions could lead to war between the colonies and Great Britain.

The colonists decided that they must stand up for themselves. On the night of December 16, 1773, a large group of colonists raided the ships in Boston Harbor. They used axes to split open the crates of tea and dump it into the sea. After all the tea had been dumped, the colonists cleaned up the ships and left.

Word of the raid spread all over New England. Many people were happy that their fellow colonists had stood up to British rule. They began to refer to the raid as "The Boston Tea Party." Great Britain retaliated by passing more laws that the colonists did not like. The colonists continued organizing themselves and protesting. Soon the colonies were at war with Great Britain, fighting for their independence.

The Boston Tea Party Flannel Board

Reproduce each of the figures below and on page 29 several times. Color the figures needed for the story and cut them out. Use blue flannel on the flannel board to indicate Boston Harbor. Then glue flannel to the backs of the figures and let children move them around the flannel board as they hear the story.

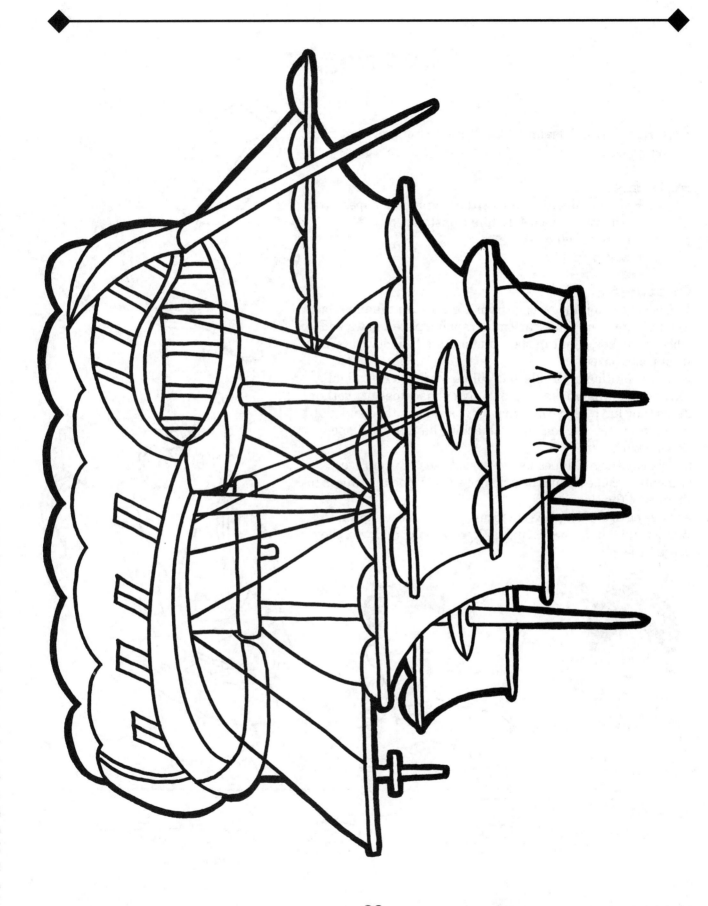

First Flight

Celebrate the anniversary of the Wright Brothers' first flight on December 17, 1903 by making these flying machines.

Materials:
- ◆ empty milk and juice cartons, wrapping paper, bows and ribbons, jar lids, film canisters, acetate
- ◆ tape and glue
- ◆ writing paper

Directions:
1. Collect clean junk garbage from the children's families such as empty milk and juice cartons, wrapping paper, bows and ribbons, jar lids, film canisters, and acetate "window coverings" from pasta boxes.
2. In celebration of Orville and Wilbur Wright's first flight, have the children make their own flying machines using the items they have been collecting. Give students tape and glue to use, and ask that each flying machine have at least one moving part.
3. Display the machines for everyone to see. Encourage students to come up and describe how their machine works to the rest of the class.
4. Give each child a piece of writing paper. Ask children to write about where they would fly if they could, and why they chose those places.

Punctuation Planes

Directions:

1. Reproduce the plane pattern on page 32 six times. On each plane, write a different punctuation symbol: question mark, period, comma, quotation marks, exclamation mark, and an apostrophe.

2. Explain to the class that each student will choose a plane, then write a sentence, question, exclamation, or quote that uses the punctuation on the plane. Have each child write the sentence on a banner created from construction paper or other material.

3. When the sentences are completed, students may attach their banners to their planes with tape or a stapler. Display the planes for everyone to see.

4. For added challenge, add some banners that do not use the punctuation symbol called for, or that use a punctuation symbol incorrectly. See if children can spot the mistakes and correct them.

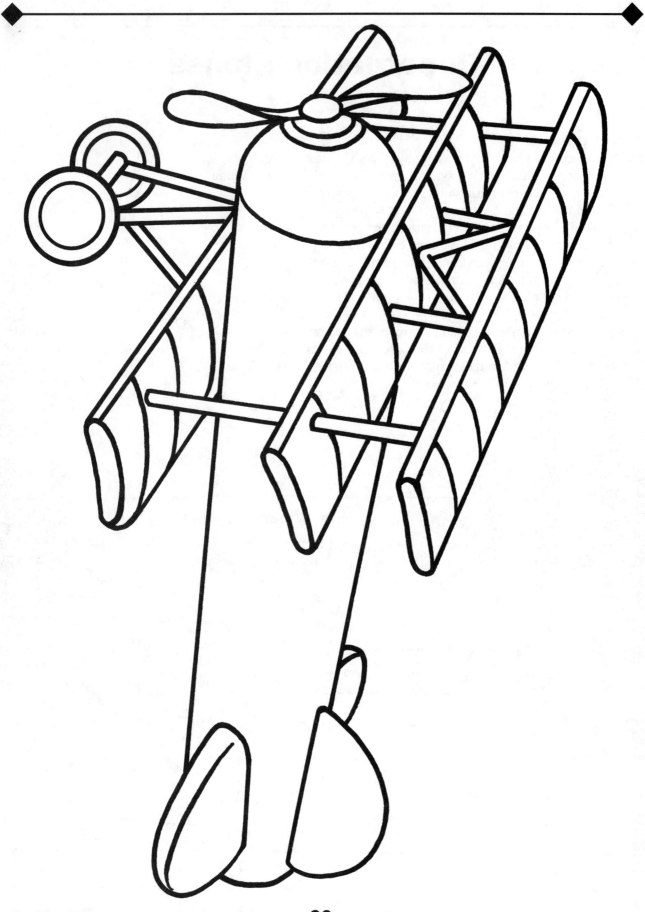

Las Posadas Piñata Party

Explain to the class that Las Posadas is a holiday celebrated in Mexico the week before Christmas. The holiday begins with a reenactment of the Bible story of Mary and Joseph's search for lodgings before the birth of Jesus. Las Posadas lasts nine days, and the celebration is eagerly awaited by Mexican children.

Tell students that the word posada means lodging. Children hold figures of Mary and Joseph and travel to a house that has been picked to be the first posada. The head of the household denies them any rooms, but upon finding out who the visitors are, invites them in to gather around the manger and sing songs.

Celebrate Las Posadas by making a piñata filled with treats for the class.

Materials:
- ◆ oaktag
- ◆ scissors
- ◆ glue
- ◆ construction paper, tissue paper, collage materials
- ◆ hole puncher
- ◆ twine
- ◆ small plastic storage bags (one for each child)
- ◆ stapler
- ◆ yarn
- ◆ masking tape
- ◆ treats (candy, small toys)

Directions:
1. Have a class vote to decide what figure the piñata will be. Encourage students to nominate different animals or objects. The nomination with the most votes will be the class piñata.

2. Trace or draw the figure onto oaktag twice. Cut out the figures, then staple the edges together, leaving very little space between the staples, as shown.

3. Sketch out the major features onto the oaktag. Lay out glue, scissors, construction paper, tissue paper, collage materials, and other materials needed for the piñata.

4. Have children decorate the piñata. For example, if the piñata calls for hair, demonstrate to children how to make slits 1/2" apart on a 3" strip of paper, stopping 1" from the other edge. These can then be glued to the piñata, starting from the bottom and overlapping slightly.

5. Add a tail to the piñata if necessary by stapling braided yarn to the back of the piñata.

6. When the piñata is completed, cut a hole in the top and place small plastic storage bags filled with treats inside.

7. Reinforce the open edges with masking tape. Then punch two holes about 1" down from the top of the piñata.

8. Loop a long piece of twine through the holes and tie the ends together, as shown. Hang the piñata from a hook in the ceiling so that it is about 18" above the children's heads.

9. Give each child a turn to hit the piñata with a plastic bat or wooden yardstick, trying to break it open. Make sure children are a safe distance away before each strike is made. When the piñata breaks open, each student may come forward and take a goodie bag.

The Story of Hanukkah

Hanukkah usually occurs in December. The name Hanukkah means "dedication" in Yiddish. It is also called the Festival of Lights.

Long ago, in 165 B.C., a group of Jewish people, called the Maccabees, fought for religious freedom. They were persecuted by a Syrian king, named Antiochus IV, who ordered his army to take their temple away.

But the Maccabees did not give up. They fought back and recovered their temple. When they gathered together again inside the temple, however, the Maccabees found that they had only enough oil to light the *Ner Tamid* (Eternal Light) for one day.

Then a miracle occurred. The oil lamp stayed lit for eight days and nights until more oil had been prepared. Today, Jewish people commemorate this miracle by lighting one candle on a Menorah for each day of Hanukkah.

Name _____

The Story of Hanukkah

After reading "The Story of Hanukkah," fill in the crossword puzzle below.

Across

1. Light candles on this
4. The Festival of Lights
6. What the word "Hanukkah" means
7. Where Jewish people worship
8. Ordered army to take away temple

Down

2. How many days the oil lamp stayed lit
3. Group of Jewish people
5. Eternal Light

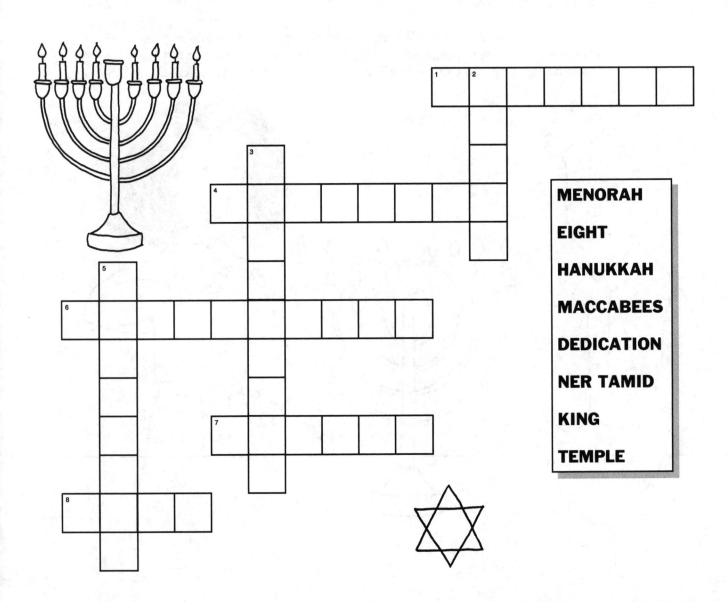

MENORAH

EIGHT

HANUKKAH

MACCABEES

DEDICATION

NER TAMID

KING

TEMPLE

Hanukkah Candles

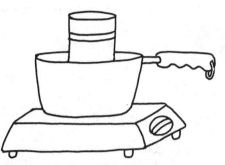

Materials:

- ◆ paraffin or old candles
- ◆ wicks from old candles or thick string, cut to desired candle height
- ◆ 2 tall tin cans (taller than candles to be made)
- ◆ pan
- ◆ hot plate
- ◆ ice water
- ◆ newspaper to cover table

Directions:

1. Pour water into a pan and set it on the hot plate. In one of the tall cans, place the paraffin and the old candles. Heat the wax on low until it melts. If necessary, add more paraffin so it comes almost to the brim. Add old crayons for color if desired.

2. While the wax is melting, fill the other can with ice water and place it on a table covered with newspaper.

3. When the paraffin has melted, take it off the heat and place it next to the ice water. Dip the string into the wax, take it out, and put in the ice water. The ice water will set the candle. Continue this procedure until the candle is the desired width.

4. Try to keep up a steady rhythm of dipping to avoid melting the previous layers. When the candle is done, hang it from the wick until it hardens completely. Then use a knife to even the bottom of the candle and trim the wick to 3/4".

5. Heat the wax again if it has cooled too long before the next child does his or her dipping. Make sure students are aware that the hot plate and wax are very hot, and that they need to be careful at all times when near them.

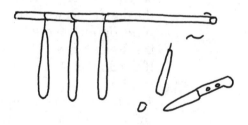

6. On the first day of Hanukkah, light the *shammos,* or main candle, and use it to light a second candle on the Menorah. Each day, use the shammos to light the previous candles plus another one, to symbolize the eight nights the oil burned.

Dreidel, Dreidel

Materials:

- crayons or markers
- glue
- oaktag
- scissors
- tape
- pencils
- playing pieces (candy, raisins, pennies)

Directions:

1. Reproduce the dreidel pattern on page 39 once for each child. Have the children color the dreidels, mount them onto oaktag, and cut them out. Punch the hole where the pencil will go.

2. Show students how to fold the dreidel along the dotted lines and tape in place.

3. Help each student gently stick a sharpened pencil through the top of the dreidel and the opposite end, so the dreidel sits in the middle of the pencil, as shown.

4. Explain to the class the significance of the symbols on the sides of the dreidel. These letters are the first letters in the words *Nes Godal, Hayah Sham,* which means "a great miracle happened here."

5. Divide the class into small groups to play the dreidel game. Each player should begin the game with a certain number of playing pieces, such as ten gold-wrapped chocolate coins, ten raisins, or ten pennies. Each player starts by placing one piece in the middle.

6. The spin of the players' dreidels will determine how the game is played. If the dreidel shows N (*Nun*), the player gets nothing and the next player goes. If the dreidel shows G (*Gimmel*), the player takes everything in the middle. If the dreidel shows H (*Hei*, pronouced "hay"), the player takes half the pieces. If the dreidel shows Sh (*Shin*), the player must put one more piece in the middle.

7. Students can continue playing for as long as they wish, or until all but one child has run out of pieces.

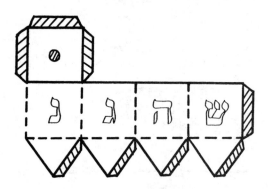

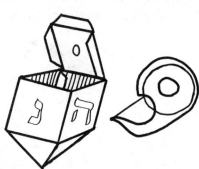

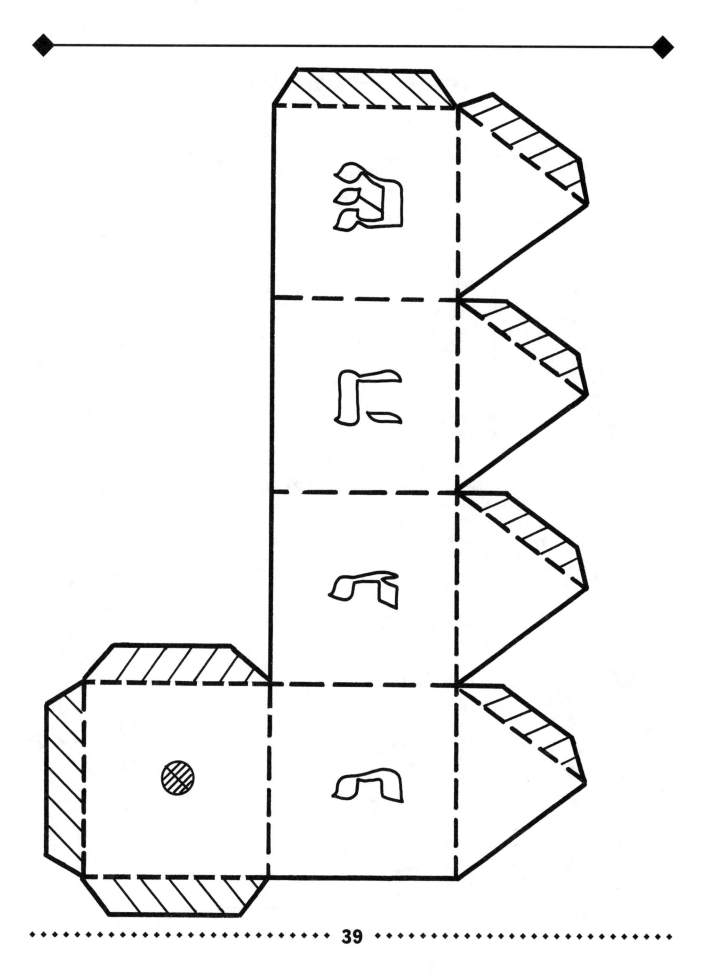

Potato Pancakes

Many people who celebrate Hanukkah make these potato pancakes, or *latkes*, to eat during the holiday. You can make them with your class by following the recipe below.

Materials:
- 10 potatoes
- 5 eggs
- 2 cups flour
- salt
- vegetable oil
- applesauce
- vegetable peeler
- blender or food processor
- electric frying pan or skillet
- paper towels
- paper plates
- plastic forks

Directions:
1. Wash the potatoes well and peel off the skins. Dry off.
2. Place the potatoes, eggs, flour, and a pinch of salt into a blender or food processor and mix well.
3. Heat oil in an electric frying pan or a skillet and drop the pancake mixture by tablespoons into the oil. Caution children to stand a safe distance away from the hot pan and oil. Fry the pancakes until golden.
4. Drain the pancakes on paper towels.
5. Serve the potato pancakes with applesauce. Enjoy!

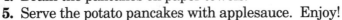

All Year Long

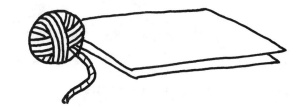

Materials:
- ◆ blank calendar
- ◆ glue
- ◆ construction paper
- ◆ crayons or markers
- ◆ clear contact paper
- ◆ hole puncher
- ◆ yarn

Directions:
1. Reproduce the months of the year from a blank calendar once for each child in the class.

2. Have children mount each month on a piece of construction paper. Let children color these pages.

3. Give each child 12 pieces of construction paper. Tell each child to draw one scene for each month of the year. For example, a child might wish to draw a picture of a Christmas tree to represent December, or a beach scene for July.

4. Help children laminate the pages of their calendars.

5. Put each calendar together in order so that each month is facing the appropriate illustration.

6. Punch approximately five holes along the top edge of the calendar. Thread yarn through the holes to sew the pages together. Then tie an 18" piece of yarn to the holes on the ends to make a hanger for the calendar.

7. The pages of the calendar should open, as shown. Have children give the calendars to their parents, grandparents, or other family members as holiday gifts.

The Very Best Gift Wrap

Materials:

◆ butcher paper
◆ tins
◆ tempera paint
◆ potatoes
◆ sponges
◆ cookie cutters

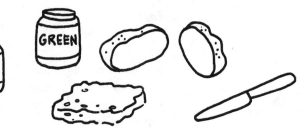

Directions:
1. Give each child a large sheet of butcher paper. On an art table, place several tins with different colors of tempera paint.
2. Wash several potatoes of varying sizes. Cut the potatoes in half lengthwise or widthwise. Carve designs into the potatoes.
3. Cut sponges into different shapes or simple figures. Use cookie cutters to trace outlines on the sponges if desired.
4. Show children how to dip the sponges and potatoes into the paint and blot them across the paper to make designs and patterns. Encourage children to superimpose various prints to create unique designs. Children may also place their hands in the tins to make handprint designs on the paper.
5. After the paint has dried, children may use the paper to wrap their holiday gifts.

Flower Paperweight

Materials:
- ◆ different colored tissue paper
- ◆ glue
- ◆ small plastic juice containers
- ◆ paintbrushes
- ◆ clear polyurethane
- ◆ pipe cleaners
- ◆ plaster mixture

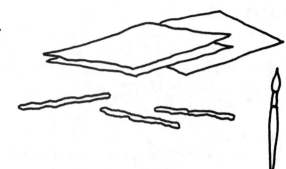

Directions:

1. Demonstrate how to tear tissue paper into small shapes and then glue them to the outside of a juice container, as shown. After the glue has dried, give the containers a coating of polyurethane.

2. To make the flowers for the paperweight, have each child begin by laying two squares or circles of tissue paper (about 5" wide) on the palm of one hand. Then have each student poke the index finger of the other hand into the middle of the layers, turning the papers upside down so now the flat palm is on top.

3. Next, show each child how to gather the paper around the index finger and remove the finger, pinching the gathered paper and turning right side up, as shown. Wrap one end of a pipe cleaner around the pinched side of the flower to complete.

4. To make a rose, fold a 3" x 12" piece of tissue paper in half lengthwise. Holding one end between the thumb and fingers of one hand, wrap the rest around the hand. Gather one end and pinch the edges together. Wrap a pipe cleaner around the gathered end. Each child should make about three or four flowers for the vase.

5. Help each student pour the plaster into each vase until it is about three-quarters full. Stick the free ends of the pipe cleaner flowers into the plaster. Hold them in place for a count of twenty, or until the plaster begins to stiffen.

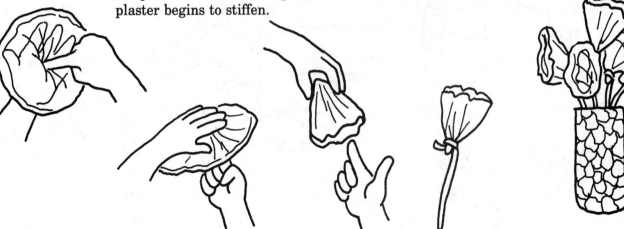

Little Handprints

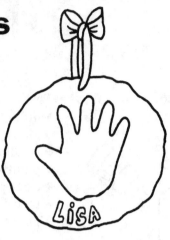

Materials:
- ◆ plaster mixture
- ◆ plastic-coated 5" plates
- ◆ vegetable oil
- ◆ unsharpened pencil
- ◆ ribbon or yarn

Directions:

1. Mix up a batch of plaster in a cup or a small bowl, enough for each child to make one handprint at a time. Pour the mixture onto a plate and even out.

2. Rub the child's hand in a small amount of vegetable oil and have that child press his or her hand into the plaster with fingers splayed. The impression should be deep enough to see, but not so deep that it goes to the plate.

3. This process must be done quickly to avoid having the plaster dry before the child is ready. If the plaster begins drying before it is in the plate, throw it out and start again. Adding more water will not make the mixture soft again.

4. After the print has been made, use an unsharpened pencil to poke a hole through to the plate.

5. When the prints are dry, let students paint their handprints. Have each child paint his or her name on the handprint. After they are finished, help each child slip a length of yarn or ribbon through the hole and tie the ends in a bow.

The Nutcracker Flannel Board Story

One Christmas Eve, long, long ago, a girl named Clara celebrated the holiday with her brother, mother, and father. That night Clara and her brother were to receive their presents.

After what seemed like a very long time, they were allowed to enter the sitting room, which was beautifully decorated with many glittering and delicate ornaments. Clara was very excited as she opened her gifts. Not only did she receive the doll she had been wishing for most, but there was a curious new toy under the tree. She picked it up and asked her godfather to tell her about the little man with the big mouth.

Godfather told her it was a nutcracker. He explained to Clara that all she had to do was put a nut in his mouth, pull down on the lever behind his neck, and the mouth would close, breaking open the nut. Clara's brother also wanted to try the nutcracker. But he pushed so hard on the lever that the mouth broke off and the teeth fell out.

Clara was sad and angry at her brother. "Just look what you've done!" she cried. "Godfather, please—can you fix him?" Godfather promised he would come the following evening and see what he could do. That night, Clara gently placed the nutcracker on her doll's bed and stayed with him.

At midnight, Clara heard terribly loud hissing and squeaking sounds. Before she knew it, mice were running all over her room, heading for the doll bed. The leader of the mice had seven heads, and on those seven heads were seven crowns.

Clara was frightened for the nutcracker, so she threw some nuts at the mice and they scampered away. But a short time later, the mice returned with even more mice. The seven-headed king led the way. Just then, to Clara's great surprise, the nutcracker got up from the bed and led the other toys in a battle against the mice. Clara helped by throwing her dresses over the mice so they could not see where they were going.

In the morning, everything was in its place. Clara tried to tell her parents what had happened, but they did not believe her. Later that evening she repeated the story to her godfather.

"So, the mouse king has found the nutcracker," her godfather said thoughtfully. And he told Clara a story about something that had happened many years ago.

It seems a girl baby was born to a king and queen. One day while the queen was making some sausage for the king, a whole family of mice came out from under the stove and began eating all the sausage meat.

The king was so angered that he called in Clara's godfather and ordered him to invent something to get rid of all the mice. The godfather managed to get rid of all the mice with the exception of the queen mouse. The angry queen mouse put a curse on the baby, so from that point on the queen and king protected the girl very carefully. When they could not watch her, they had ten nannies to look after her.

But one day the queen fell asleep while watching the baby, and the queen mouse got into the baby's crib. When the queen woke up, the baby had turned into an ugly wooden nutcracker.

The king and queen discovered that the only way to break the spell was to find a young man who had always worn boots and never shaved. This man was to crack open a special nut for the princess so she could eat the kernel inside it. After, he had to walk backwards without falling for seven paces. The man who could do this was the godfather's nephew. However, in walking backward, the queen mouse dashed out and tripped him. Immediately the princess became her old self again and the nephew became an ugly wooden nutcracker. The only way he could become himself again was to kill the mouse queen's son, the seven-headed mouse king, and have a young girl fall in love with him.

Clara truly believed that her nutcracker was her godfather's nephew. A few nights later, she again heard a great battle raging in the sitting room. She ran in to help the nutcracker, but he had already killed the mouse king. He was halfway to becoming a man again!

Ten years passed uneventfully. One day Clara's parents were cleaning out the closets and came across the nutcracker. They tossed him aside just as Clara came into the room. She shouted, "Please leave the nutcracker alone! I love him!"

Just then the nutcracker transformed into the godfather's nephew. The two conditions to break the spell had been fulfilled: he had killed the mouse king, and a young girl had fallen in love with him. The nephew asked Clara to marry him, and they lived happily ever after.

The Nutcracker Flannel Board Story

Reproduce each of the figures below. Color the figures and cut them out. Glue flannel to the backs of the figures and let children move them around a flannel board as they hear the story.

Holiday Party Time

Have a class party to celebrate winter holidays. Help children make the following treats to serve at the party.

SUGAR COOKIES

Materials:
- 1/2 cup butter
- 1 cup sugar
- 1 beaten egg
- 1/4 cup milk
- 1/4 teaspoon vanilla
- 2 cups flour
- 2 teaspoons baking powder

Directions:
1. Leave butter out for a while to soften. Then cream the butter and sugar together.
2. Beat in the egg, milk, and vanilla. Mix well.
3. Mix the baking powder with 1 cup of the flour. Combine this mixture with the butter mixture. Then add the rest of the flour.
4. Cover the dough and chill for about one hour. Roll out on a floured surface until the dough is 1/4" thick.
5. Use cookie cutters or plastic knives to cut out shapes. Place the shapes on a cookie sheet and bake at 375°F for 8 to 10 minutes.

SNOW CONES

Directions:

1. Give children large ice cubes to shave against the side of a grater with round holes. Caution children to use a new ice cube when their fingers come too close to the grater as the old cube decreases in size. (You may also wish to place ice cubes in a sealed plastic bag and crush them with a hammer.)
2. Give each child a cone-shaped paper cup. You can make these by rolling one corner of a square piece of sturdy paper to the opposite corner, then gently widening one side and taping in place. You may also wish to line the insides of the cups with wax paper.
3. Help children scoop the shaved ice into their cups. Provide different flavorings (such as cherry juice, orange juice, and so on) for children to use to flavor their ices. Instruct children to pour a small amount on the ice in the cups.

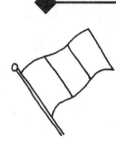
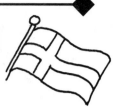

Christmas Around the World

Tell students that Christmas is celebrated all over the world, but people have a different way of saying it. Here's how you say "Merry Christmas" in these countries:

Happy Christmas–*England*

Joyeux Noël–*France* (zwa-YEUH no-EL)

Feliz Navidad–*Mexico, Spain* (feh-LEES na-vi-DOD)

God Jul–*Sweden* (gud U-el)

Buon Natale–*Italy* (BWON na-TA-leh)

Beannachtai na Nollag–*Ireland* (ban-ACT-tea nah null-OG)

Gelukkig Kerstfeest–*Netherlands* (ghe-LUK-ig KERST-fest)

Hauskaa Joulua–*Finland* (HAUS-ka U-loo-ah)

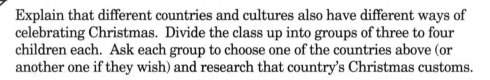

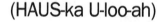

Explain that different countries and cultures also have different ways of celebrating Christmas. Divide the class up into groups of three to four children each. Ask each group to choose one of the countries above (or another one if they wish) and research that country's Christmas customs.

After each group has completed its research, ask them to make a presentation for the rest of the class. Encourage students to include songs, crafts, decorations, and food (if possible) in their presentations.

Christmas Ornaments

Materials:
- ◆ 3 cups flour
- ◆ 3 cups salt
- ◆ 1 tablespoon vegetable oil
- ◆ 1 cup of water (approximate)
- ◆ wooden spoon
- ◆ large mixing bowl
- ◆ tempera paint
- ◆ wax paper
- ◆ Christmas cookie cutters
- ◆ 6" lengths of yarn

Directions:
1. Have students help mix together the flour, salt, and oil in a large mixing bowl. Slowly add in as much water as necessary (approximately 1 cup) to give the mixture a dough-like consistency.

2. Separate the dough into different piles. Mix a different color paint into each pile. Leave one pile white if desired.

3. Have each child take a small piece of dough to use as a background color. Help the children roll the dough flat until it is about 1/4" thick on pieces of wax paper.

4. Provide the children with Christmas cookie cutters to use to make the figures. Older children may wish to use a small knife to cut out their own figures or designs.

5. Have students use different colors of the dough to add features and designs to their figures. If the dough becomes too dry, have children wet their fingers and rub a tiny bit of water on the dough.

6. Use a pencil to make a hole at the top of each figure.

7. To complete the ornaments, have each child string a 6" piece of yarn through the hole and tie together to make a loop for hanging.

8. Allow two days for the ornaments to completely dry. Stress to students that the ornaments are not to be eaten.

Christmas Card

Materials:
- ◆ crayons or markers
- ◆ scissors
- ◆ construction paper
- ◆ glue

Directions:
1. Reproduce the Christmas figures on page 53 once for each child. Have students color the figures and cut them out.

2. Ask each child to fold a 9"x 12" piece of paper in half widthwise. Glue one of the pictures to the front of the card.

3. Encourage the children to draw a scene or decorations around the animals.

4. Have each student write special Christmas messages to the recipient of the card before signing his or her own name.

Antonym Wreath Activity

1. Reproduce the wreath pattern on page 55 twice for each child. Have students color the wreaths and cut them out.
2. To begin the antonym game, write pairs of antonyms randomly around the chalkboard. Then ask volunteers to come to the board with their wreaths and encircle pairs of antonyms. Continue until all the pairs have been found.
3. You may also wish to play this game using synonyms. Place a wreath around one of a pair of synonyms, and ask a volunteer to find its match.

Christmas Stocking

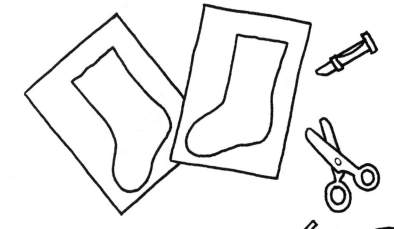

Materials:
- ◆ oaktag pattern of stocking
- ◆ flannel
- ◆ marker
- ◆ hole punch
- ◆ embroidery thread or yarn
- ◆ blunt needles
- ◆ scissors
- ◆ glitter on a paper plate

Directions:
1. Trace an oaktag stocking pattern four times. In groups of four to five children each, demonstrate how to trace the pattern onto two pieces of oaktag using a marker.
2. Help each child punch holes about 1" apart along the edges of the stocking, leaving the top intact.
3. Have each child tie one end of a 3' length of thread or yarn into the first hole nearest the top of the stocking. Then thread 6" of the other end through the eye of the needle, as shown.
4. Demonstrate to students how to insert the needle into the next hole, pull the thread out the back until taut, and continue sewing in and out until the last hole is reached.
5. Help each child knot the end of the thread into the last hole.
6. Ask each student to cut a scrap of flannel wide enough to cover the top of the stocking and glue it to the front top of the stocking, as shown.
7. Have each child write his or her name in glue on this flannel scrap. Then let each child shake glitter over the glue until it is completely covered. After the glue has dried, shake each stocking gently to remove the excess glitter.

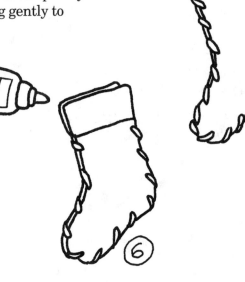

Name _____

Holiday Shopping

Taylor wants to buy holiday gifts for his mom, dad, older sister, and baby brother. He has **$70.00** to spend for all four gifts. Help Taylor choose gifts for his family from the items in the shop. Use the space below to add up the cost for each item you buy. Remember, Taylor can't spend more than **$70.00**!

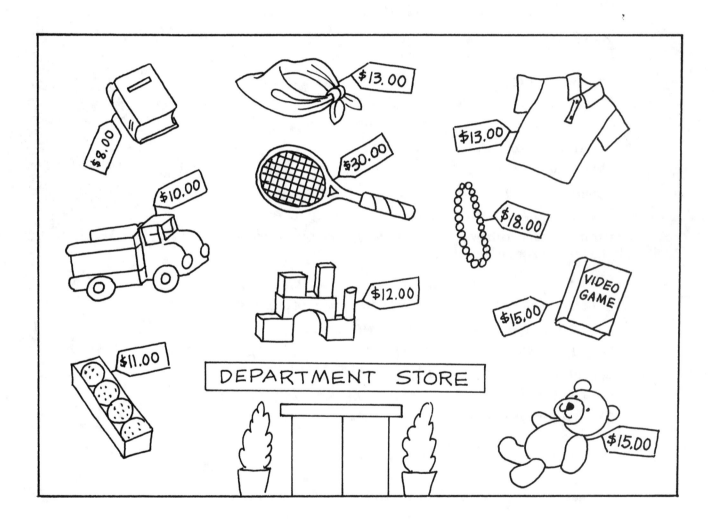

How much money does Taylor have left? _____

Twelve Days of Christmas

On the first day of Christmas, my true love gave to me,
A partridge in a pear tree.
On the second day of Christmas, my true love gave to me,
Two turtledoves, and a partridge in a pear tree.
On the third day of Christmas, my true love gave to me,
Three French hens, two turtledoves, and a partridge in a pear tree.
On the fourth day of Christmas, my true love gave to me,
Four calling birds, three French hens,...
On the fifth day of Christmas, my true love gave to me,
Five golden rings, four calling birds,...
On the sixth day of Christmas, my true love gave to me,
Six geese a-laying, five golden rings,...
On the seventh day of Christmas, my true love gave to me,
Seven swans a-swimming, six geese a-laying,...
On the eighth day of Christmas, my true love gave to me,
Eight maids a-milking, seven swans a-swimming,...
On the ninth day of Christmas, my true love gave to me,
Nine ladies dancing, eight maids a-milking,...
On the tenth day of Christmas, my true love gave to me,
Ten lords a-leaping, nine ladies dancing,...
On the eleventh day of Christmas, my true love gave to me,
Eleven pipers piping, ten lords a-leaping,...
On the twelfth day of Christmas, my true love gave to me,
Twelve drummers drumming, eleven pipers piping,...

1. Teach students the words to this traditional Christmas song. Then ask the children to make up their own songs featuring things they would like to give or receive for the 12 days of Christmas.
2. Ask each child to write or dictate his or her song and provide an illustration.
3. Attach the songs and illustrations on a bulletin board under the heading "The 12 Days of Christmas."

Best Books About Christmas

◆ *Father Christmas*, by Raymond Briggs (Puffin, 1977)

◆ *Christmas in the Barn*, by Margaret Wise Brown (HarperCollins, 1985)

◆ *Little Christmas Elf*, by Eileen Curran (Troll, 1985)

◆ *Babar and Father Christmas*, by Jean De Brunhoff (Knopf, 1990)

◆ *Jingle the Christmas Clown*, by Tomie de Paola (Putnam, 1992)

◆ *Merry Christmas, Strega Nona*, by Tomie de Paola (Harcourt Brace, 1986)

◆ *Christmas in Noisy Village*, by Astrid Lindgren (Puffin, 1981)

◆ *Teeny Witch and the Christmas Magic*, by Liz Matthews (Troll, 1991)

◆ *Merry Christmas, Amelia Bedelia*, by Peggy Parish (Greenwillow, 1986)

◆ *Santa's New Sled*, by Sharon Peters (Troll, 1981)

◆ *Henry and Mudge in the Sparkle Days*, by Cynthia Rylant (Macmillan, 1988)

◆ *The Puppy Who Wanted a Boy*, by Jane Thayer (Morrow, 1986)

◆ *The Polar Express*, by Chris Van Allsburg (Houghton-Mifflin, 1985)

◆ *The Horrible Holidays*, by Audrey Wood (Dial, 1988)

Boxing Day

Boxing Day is celebrated in England and Canada on the first weekday after Christmas. It is said to have started when aristocratic people boxed up presents to give to their servants. Today people often celebrate Boxing Day by giving cards, gifts, or money to community workers to thank them for their work all year.

Talk about the community workers who help us every day in school. Ask students to discuss the kinds of jobs there are in school, and what responsibilities and skills each job requires of the worker.

Encourage students to celebrate Boxing Day by making cards or small gifts for school workers, such as the librarian, the principal, cafeteria workers, and the school nurse. Put each collection of cards or gifts in a box and wrap it with plain brown paper to give it an old-fashioned look. Let children decorate the paper using crayons or markers.

A Kwanzaa Celebration

Inform children that many African Americans celebrate Kwanzaa, a holiday that began in the United States in the 1960's. Kwanzaa celebrates African culture and the values of family and community.

Red, green, and black are the colors of Kwanzaa. Homes are decorated with objects of these colors, which symbolize different things: red symbolizes the bloodshed and continuing struggle of African American people; green symbolizes the green of Africa and the future hopes and dreams of African Americans; and black symbolizes the skin color of African Americans.

The festival is celebrated for seven days, from December 26 through January 1, and emphasizes a different principle each day—unity, self-determination, group responsibility, group economics, purpose, creativity, and faith. Each night, families gather to light a candle on the kinara, or candleholder, and talk about one of the seven principles. Throughout the seven days, children may receive presents. These gifts are usually cultural items, books, or homemade things, reflecting the principles of Kwanzaa.

Display books about African culture for the class to review. Then distribute red, green, and black paper, collage materials, and other items to students. Ask the children to create masks resembling those made in Africa. Children may also wish to make their own Kwanzaa cards or other Kwanzaa gifts.

Happy New Year Party Favor

Materials:

- ◆ cardboard toilet-paper rolls
- ◆ tissue paper
- ◆ collage materials
- ◆ stickers
- ◆ glue
- ◆ small trinkets and candies
- ◆ curling ribbon

Directions:

1. Distribute one cardboard toilet-paper roll and one piece of tissue paper to each child. Lay out pans of different collage materials, stickers, and glue for each student to use to decorate one side of the paper.

2. Let each child choose three trinkets and candies. Ask children to place these items inside the rolls.

3. Tell students to lay the tissue paper decorated sides down. Then have each child slowly roll the cardboard roll over the paper, as shown. Tape the paper closed.

4. Help each student gather the tissue paper together about 1" away from the end of the roll on both sides. Tie each end with curling ribbon, leaving a puff on each end, as shown.

5. Place the party favors in a bag and have each student close his or her eyes and choose one. When everyone has received a favor, have the class shout, "Happy New Year!" and open them for New Year treats.

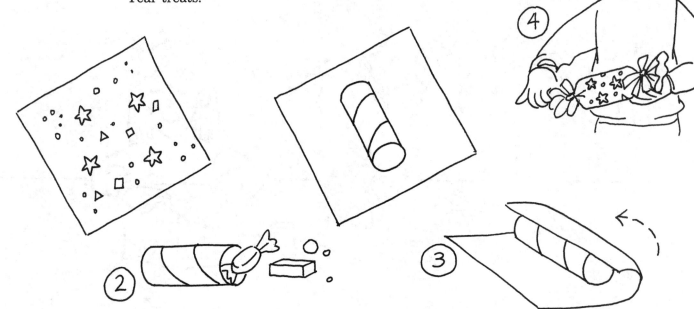

What A Year!

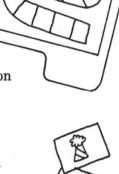

Play this file-folder game with the class to review things that have happened during the year.

Materials:
- ◆ crayons or markers
- ◆ scissors
- ◆ glue
- ◆ letter-sized file folder
- ◆ clear contact paper
- ◆ different-colored construction paper
- ◆ envelope

Directions:
1. Reproduce the game board on pages 64-65 once. Reproduce the game cards on page 66 two times. Color all the materials and cut them out.

2. Glue the game board to the inside of a letter-sized file folder.

3. Write various types of situations that have happened to your class during the year on the backs of half of the game cards. For example, you may write, "We go on a field trip to the museum," or "Our science experiment doesn't work!" Assign a number (+1, +2, -1, -2) to each card based upon the situation (such as +2 for the museum card, and -2 for each science experiment card).

4. Write the words "Pass" or "Lose a Turn" on three cards. Write a number from one to three on the remainder of the cards.

5. Laminate all the playing cards. Then cut four 1″ squares from scraps of different colored construction paper to make playing pieces. Laminate these pieces as well.

6. Glue an envelope to the back of the file folder for storage of game cards and playing pieces.

7. Reproduce the Game Rules and glue them to the front of the file folder.

Game Rules (for 2 to 4 players)
1. Shuffle the game cards and place them facedown on the game board. Place the playing pieces at "Start."

2. The youngest player goes first and chooses a card. That player proceeds according to the directions on the card. For example, if a number is on the card, the player will move ahead that number of spaces on the game board. If a situation is on the card, the player will move ahead or back as many spaces as indicated, or lose a turn if he or she has drawn that card. If a "Pass" card is drawn, the player may save it to get out of moving backward or losing a turn.

3. The first player to reach "Finish" is the winner.

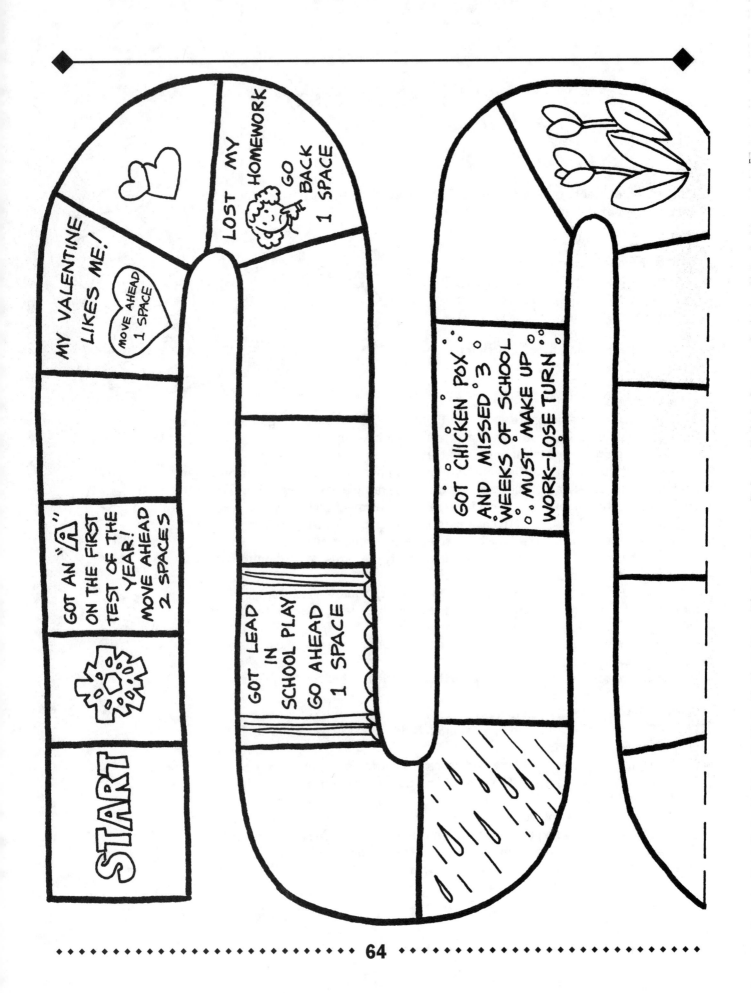

START

MY VALENTINE LIKES ME!
MOVE AHEAD 1 SPACE

GOT AN "A" ON THE FIRST TEST OF THE YEAR! MOVE AHEAD 2 SPACES

LOST MY HOMEWORK
GO BACK 1 SPACE

GOT LEAD IN SCHOOL PLAY GO AHEAD 1 SPACE

GOT CHICKEN POX AND MISSED 3 WEEKS OF SCHOOL. MUST MAKE UP WORK—LOSE TURN

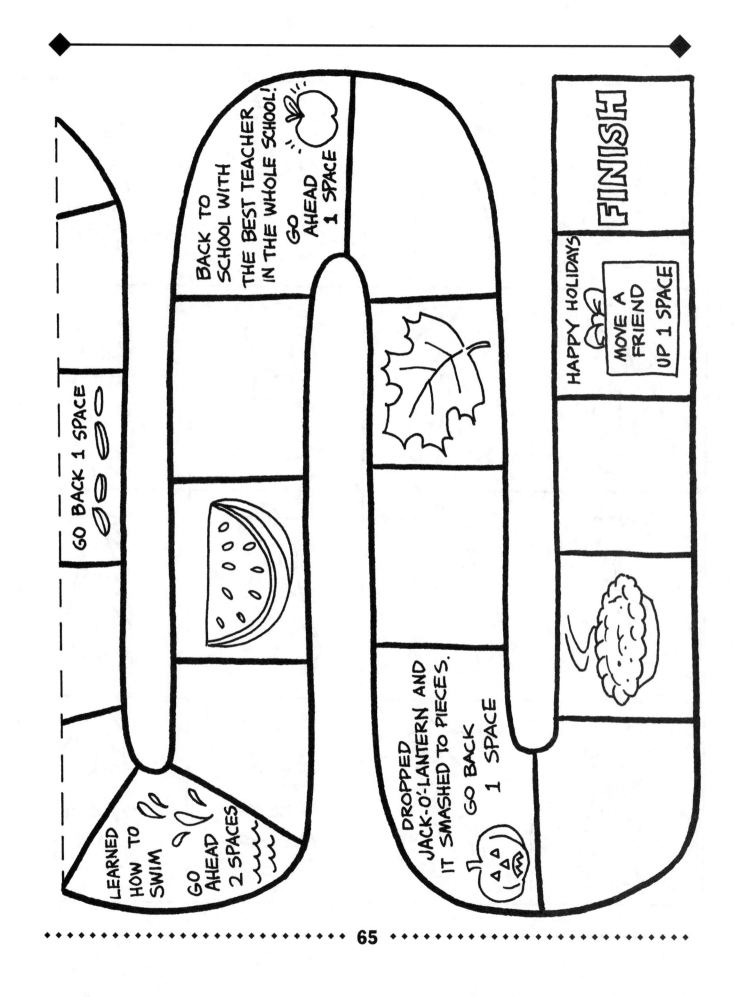

LEARNED HOW TO SWIM GO AHEAD 2 SPACES

GO BACK 1 SPACE

BACK TO SCHOOL WITH THE BEST TEACHER IN THE WHOLE SCHOOL! GO AHEAD 1 SPACE

DROPPED JACK-O'-LANTERN AND IT SMASHED TO PIECES. GO BACK 1 SPACE

HAPPY HOLIDAYS MOVE A FRIEND UP 1 SPACE

FINISH

Happy Birthday, Betsy Ross!

Betsy Ross was born on January 1, 1752. Explain to students that Betsy Ross is generally credited with sewing the first flag for the American colonies in 1776. There were thirteen stars and stripes to symbolize the thirteen colonies at that time. On June 14, 1777, the Congress accepted her design and it became the flag of the United States of America.

In 1818 a law was passed to create a new star for each new state, while leaving the 13 stripes unchanged to represent the original thirteen colonies. The American flag now has fifty stars to represent the fifty states. Ask the class if anyone knows which state was the last to join the Union. (Hawaii.)

Have students create their own countries where they are the heads of the governments and make the rules and decisions. Encourage them to describe their countries: climate, geography, economics, people, holidays, food, recreation, and laws. When the children are finished writing their descriptions, distribute paper, scissors, glue, and other collage materials so that they may make flags that symbolize things about their countries.

Display the flags on a bulletin board for everyone to see. Let students attach their country's "charters" below them for all to read and share.

Physically Challenged People

Louis Braille was born on January 4, 1809. He was able to see when he was young, but he soon became blind in an accident in his father's workshop.

When Braille was twenty years old, he published a system of reading and writing for blind people. Before that time there had not been a way for blind people to read or write by themselves. Braille used a system of raised dots, with each combination symbolizing a different number or letter.

Discuss with the class the special challenges presented to people who have lost the ability to use a limb or one of their senses. If possible, invite someone who is physically challenged into the classroom to speak to children about how they meet everyday challenges that we might take for granted. Then take a walk around the school and talk about possible hazards or benefits for people in wheelchairs. Does the school provide ramps or flat walkways and entrances? If your building has more than one story, are there elevators? Are telephones and drinking fountains accessible for the handicapped?

Try the following experiments with the class to help students get an idea of what it is like trying to cope with a handicap:

◆ Ask the children to drop beans into a cup while blindfolded.
◆ Have students tie their shoes with socks over their hands.
◆ Tell the class to hold their noses while tasting a food blindfolded.
◆ Ask students to walk across the room using only one leg.
◆ Have each child find an object from the cabinet while blindfolded.
◆ Tell each student to write a word on a piece of paper without using their fingers.

Discuss how students felt and how they coped during these experiments. Encourage the class to feel compassion and understanding for people who are the same as we are but physically challenged.

Best Books About the Physically Challenged

◆ *I'm Deaf and It's Okay*, Lorraine Aseltine (Whitman, 1986)

◆ *On Our Own Terms: Children Living with Physical Handicaps; Seeing in Special Ways: Children Living with Blindness; We Laugh, We Love, We Cry: Children Living with Mental Retardation*, all by Thomas Bergman (Gareth Stevens, 1989)

◆ *Someone Special, Just Like You*, by Tricia Brown (Holt, 1984)

◆ *The Mystery of the Boy Next Door*, by Elizabeth Montgomery (Garrad, 1978)

◆ *My Sister's Special*, by Jo Prall (Childrens Press, 1985)

◆ *See You Tomorrow, Charles*, by Charles Cohen (Dell, 1989)

◆ *Fanny*, by Stephen Cosgrove (Price Stern Sloan, 1986)

Learning About Others

Dr. Martin Luther King, Jr. was born on January 15, 1929. He had a dream that one day all people would live together in peace and happiness. One way to encourage children to follow in Dr. King's footsteps is by fighting prejudice about others who may look, speak, or behave differently.

Design a form asking children's parents and relatives to contribute songs, poems, stories, recipes, costumes, musical instruments, or pictures that reflect their cultural heritage. Ask them to describe the cultures from which their contributions originate.

Have a class "Multicultural Party." Hang posters on the wall displaying children's drawings of all types of people working and playing together. Borrow albums from the library that reflect the cultural makeup of the class, as well as some with which children may not be familiar.

Make refreshments for the party by following recipes suggested by parents that emphasize their various ancestries. Teach the children a simple folk dance to perform for the guests at the party. You may also wish to teach children a song in another language to sing at the party. If possible, have parents come in to help with the preparations.

When all the party preparations have been made, invite families and school members to come, sampling all the foods and music, and enjoying the entertainment.

Read All About It!

Celebrate Benjamin Franklin's birthday (January 17, 1706) by helping students set up a class newsletter. Divide the class into several groups—photographers, reporters, editors, art designers, cartoonists, delivery people, and so on. Explain and discuss the different responsibilities each job has. (Students may need to do more than one job for the newsletter.)

Have a class discussion to decide which topics should be covered in the newsletter. Some topics may be introducing a new student or teacher, debating the school dress code, announcing any special events or trips, reviewing current films, books, or television shows for children, or reporting on field trips or guests to the classroom. The class should also suggest names for the newsletter and take a vote to select one.

Give the reporters, editors, photographers, and artists a week to put their stories together. Then present the stories to the designers to lay out in newspaper form on pieces of photocopy paper. When the newspaper is completed to everyone's satisfaction, reproduce it as many times as necessary for the "subscribers" in the school, and once for each child to take home. Then let the delivery people distribute the papers.

Afterwards, discuss the process of making the newsletter. Ask students to talk about the parts of their jobs they liked and disliked. If possible, invite a representative from a local paper to come to the classroom to answer questions students may have.

Presidential Terms

Inauguration Day falls on January 20 every four years. Draw lines to match each president with the years he served in office.

1. John F. Kennedy	1953-61
2. Thomas Jefferson	1981-89
3. Ronald Reagan	1933-45
4. George Washington	1961-63
5. Franklin D. Roosevelt	1861-65
6. Theodore Roosevelt	1789-97
7. John Adams	1977-81
8. Abraham Lincoln	1801-09
9. Dwight D. Eisenhower	1901-09
10. Jimmy Carter	1797-1801

Feel the Beat!

1. Celebrate Wolfgang Amadeus Mozart's birthday (January 27, 1756) by collecting different kinds of music for the children to listen to in the classroom: classical, jazz, rock, rap, opera, folk, symphony, ragtime band, blues, pop, country. Play a different genre each day, or play one type in the morning and another in the afternoon.

2. Ask the class for comments about how the music makes them feel, or what it reminds them of. Try to match activities to different types of music. (For example, symphony may be just right for rest time, but a ragtime band might be good for a party.)

3. Distribute paper and crayons or paint and encourage children to draw how the music makes them feel as they listen to it.

4. Ask volunteers to show the class how they would move or dance to the different types of music.

Name _____

Musical Messages

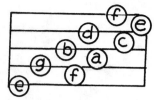

Write the letter of each musical note on the line provided to find out what this note says.

_ _ _ _ R   _ _ _ ,

_ _ _ _ _ TH _ O _

_ _ _ _ O R _ _ _ .

_ _

© 1994 Troll Associates

Chinese New Year Decorations

Red is thought to be a lucky color among Chinese, especially at the New Year, which occurs during the first new moon between January 21 and February 19. Many Chinese decorate their houses with red objects and give red envelopes filled with treats or money to children.

Celebrate Chinese New Year with the class by making these lanterns.

Materials:

- ◆ 12" x 18" red construction paper
- ◆ scissors
- ◆ tape

Directions:

1. Give each child a piece of 12" x 18" red construction paper. Show them how to fold it in half lengthwise.

2. Starting 1" in from the side, cut slits 1" apart on the folded edge to 1" from the free edges. Remember to leave 1" at the other side.

3. Open the paper and fold in half widthwise. Then tape the paper closed.

4. Have students cut strips of 2" x 6" red paper for the handle. Tape these strips to opposite sides of the top of the lantern.

5. Hang the lanterns from the classroom ceiling for a festive atmosphere.

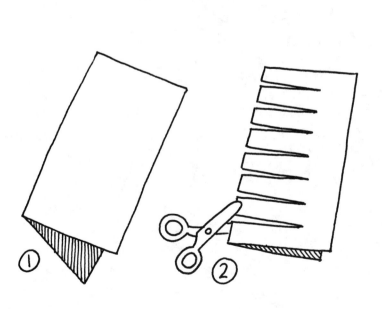

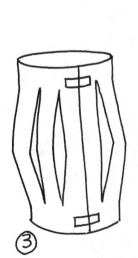

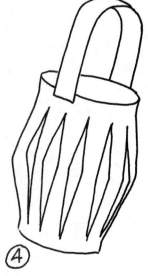

Lucky Red Envelopes

Materials:
- crayons or markers
- scissors
- tape
- small treats or coins

Directions:
1. Reproduce the envelope pattern on page 77 once for each child. Have students color the envelopes red and the dragons any colors they choose.
2. Demonstrate how to fold the sections to form an envelope. Fold section 3 over toward section 2 along the dotted lines. Then repeat with section 4, as shown.
3. Tape section 3 to 4 and section 2 to 4, as shown.
4. Fold down the top flap along the dotted lines, but do not close it. Let students fill the envelopes with small treats or coins before taping them shut.
5. Encourage the children to give their envelopes to family members or friends.

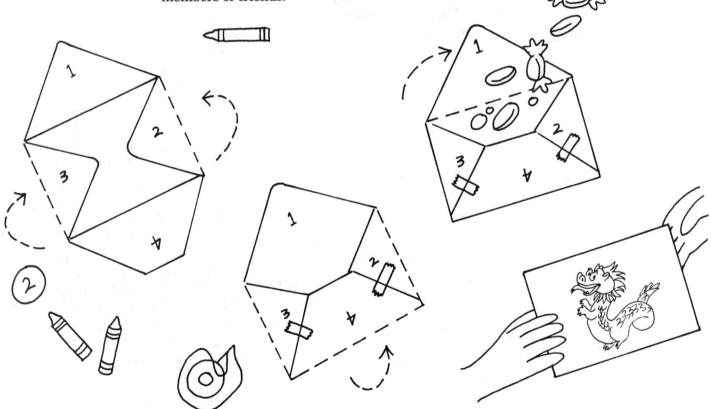

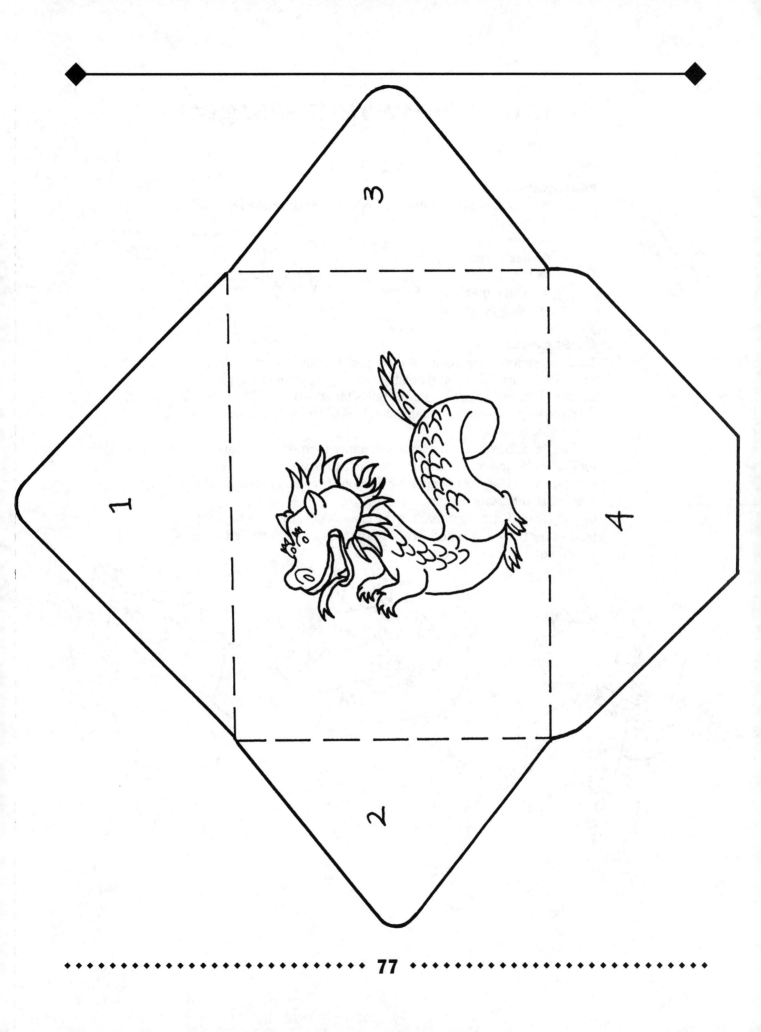

Chinese New Year Dragon

Materials:

- empty, clean, cardboard boxes (approximately 18" x 18")
- scissors
- crayons or markers
- construction paper
- glue
- collage materials
- tissue paper

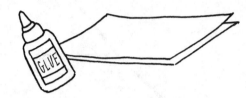

Directions:

1. Have each child bring in an empty, clean box approximately 18" x 18" in size. (It should be large enough to fit over a child's head.) Help each student cut out holes for the eyes and the mouth.

2. Encourage students to make sketches of what they want their dragons to look like.

3. Let the children use construction paper to make eyes, nose, tongue, ears, and other features for their dragons.

4. Show the class how to give the dragons texture by using collage materials and tissue paper.

5. Play some Chinese music for the class. Ask students to place the boxes over their heads and dance to the music to celebrate Chinese New Year.

Famous African Americans Class Presentations

During February, which is Black History Month, write a list of acclaimed African Americans, past and present, on a chalkboard. Be sure to write down as many names as there are students in the class. Gather the class together and briefly describe what each person has accomplished, and why that person is renowned.

Assign one of the African Americans to each student. Have the children use library and classroom materials to write a short biography of each person. Ask each child to draw a picture of a scene from each person's life to accompany the biography.

When all the biographies have been completed, ask each student to present the story of his or her historical figure to the rest of the class. Encourage students to ask questions about each person, and help the children answer these questions.

After the presentations have been made, gather together the biographies and illustrations. Staple them to a bulletin board under the title, "Black History Month."

Suggestions for biographies:

BLACK HISTORY MONTH

◆ Hank Aaron

◆ Arthur Ashe

◆ Ralph Bunche

◆ George Washington Carver

◆ Shirley Chisholm

◆ Frederick Douglass

◆ Dr. Charles Richard Drew

◆ W.E.B. DuBois

◆ Duke Ellington

◆ Marcus Garvey

◆ Alex Haley

◆ Langston Hughes

◆ Dr. Martin Luther King, Jr.

◆ Thurgood Marshall

◆ Willie Mays

◆ Toni Morrison

◆ Jesse Owens

◆ Rosa Parks

◆ Jackie Robinson

◆ Harriet Tubman

◆ Alice Walker

◆ Phillis Wheatley

◆ Malcolm X

◆ Andrew Young

Name _____

Take Care of Your Teeth

Unscramble these words about dental health.

msug   _____

rfeiould   _____

hubttrohso   _____

ofssl   _____

esttthaopo   _____

vycita   _____

ngllfii   _____

srmloa   _____

ebti   _____

tndiset   _____

Groundhog Puppet

Tell the class that there is a legend that says that if the groundhog comes out of his or her burrow and stays outside, winter will be shorter than usual. If the groundhog goes back inside the burrow, there will be six more weeks of winter. Every year on February 2, many people watch to see what their local groundhog will do.

Materials:

◆ brown construction paper
◆ scissors
◆ crayons or markers
◆ glue
◆ craft sticks
◆ large plastic cups
◆ tape

Directions:
1. Distribute brown paper to the children and help them cut out the figure of a groundhog approximately 4" in height, as shown. Lay out crayons or markers so that students may add facial and body features to their puppets.
2. Glue a craft stick to the back of each groundhog.
3. Give each child a large plastic cup. Wrap brown paper around the cup and tape in place to make the burrow opening.
4. Cut a slit in the bottom of the cup wide enough for the craft stick to fit through. Place the bottom of the craft stick into the hole from the inside of the cup. The puppet should be able to sit on the bottom of the cup sticking out over the top.
5. Show students how to push up on the craft sticks to make their groundhogs come out of the burrows, and pull down on the craft sticks to make their groundhogs hurry back into their homes.

Log Cabin Homes

Make these log cabins with the class on Abraham Lincoln's birthday, February 12.

Materials:
- ◆ scissors
- ◆ brown construction paper
- ◆ clean, empty, pint-sized milk containers
- ◆ glue
- ◆ shiny pennies
- ◆ crayons or markers

Directions:
1. Help each student cut a strip of brown construction paper wide enough to be wrapped around a milk container and tall enough to cover the sides. Glue in place.
2. Tell the children to use crayons or markers to make lines on the paper to resemble log cabins.
3. To make the roof, help each child cut a strip of construction paper wide enough to cover the slanted top of the container. Glue in place.
4. To make the front door, have each student cut a piece of paper and fold it in half, then glue it to the front of the cabin, as shown. Students may also wish to cut smaller pieces of paper to make windows to glue around the cabin.
5. Give each child a shiny penny to glue in the doorway or window to make it appear as though Abraham Lincoln were looking out of his cabin.

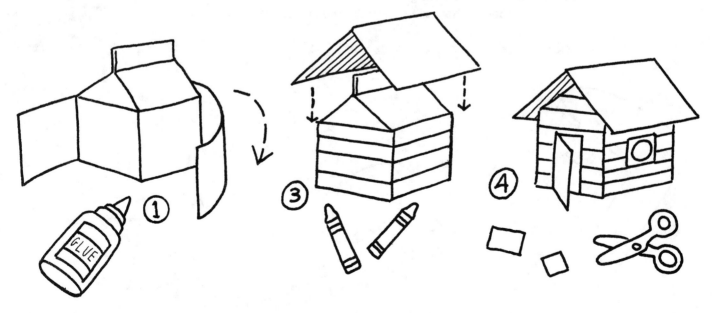

Name _____

Emancipation Proclamation

The Civil War divided the United States between the southern states of the Confederacy, which supported the system of slavery, and the northern states of the Union, which wanted to abolish slavery. This war began after the 11 southern states that formed the Confederacy seceded from the Union in 1860-61.

On January 1, 1863, after several years of war, President Abraham Lincoln issued the Emancipation Proclamation. This document proclaimed freedom for all slaves in the states held by the Confederacy. It also allowed for the northern Union to use African Americans in the Union Army and Navy.

With African Americans helping out, the Union soon won the war. By the time the Civil War was over, over a half million African Americans had escaped to freedom in the Union-held states.

On December 18, 1865, the 13th Amendment, which ended slavery in all parts of the United States, was added to the Constitution.

Write definitions for the following words.

1. slavery _____

2. abolish _____

3. secede _____

4. emancipate _____

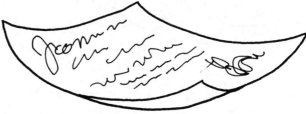

Valentine's Day Legend

1. Have a class discussion about Valentine's Day. Tell students that people believe Valentine's Day started in different ways. Some people think that it began hundreds of years ago when a Roman emperor forbade young men to get married. The emperor thought the young men would make better soldiers if they were not married. A priest named Valentine felt sorry for the young men who wanted to get married, so he secretly defied this order and married many young couples.

2. Ask the children to tell how they celebrate Valentine's Day. Tell the class that Valentine's Day is celebrated all over the world. In Great Britain, children sing Valentine's Day songs and receive candy or money. In Denmark, friends exchange snowdrops, which are pressed white flowers. Unmarried women in Italy stand by their windows at sunrise, watching for men to pass. The custom says that the first man a woman sees will marry her that year. And in Ireland, men give women claddaghs, which symbolize friendship and love.

3. Reproduce the valentine card patterns on page 85 once for each child. Have students color the cards and cut them out.

4. Ask the children to trace the cards on construction paper and cut out again.

5. Staple the cards along the left sides.

6. Tell students to make up Valentine's Day poems to write inside their cards. Encourage each child to think up a special custom to celebrate Valentine's Day in a unique way.

Valentine's Day Brooch

Materials:

- 1 cup cornstarch
- 2 cups baking soda
- 1 1/4 cups water
- flour
- medium-sized pot
- wooden spoon
- plastic knives
- cookie cutters
- paint and paintbrushes
- polyurethane or shellac
- craft glue
- safety pins
- tissue paper
- ribbons

Directions:

1. Combine the cornstarch and baking soda in a medium-sized pot.
2. Gradually add water, stirring until the mixture is smooth.
3. Cook over medium heat, stirring constantly, until the mixture has thickened and has a dough-like consistency.
4. Place mixture on a floured surface and knead well.
5. Roll out the dough so it measures 1/4" thick. The children may then cut out Valentine's Day shapes using plastic knives or cookie cutters.
6. Have students leave the dough out to dry thoroughly. When dry, let the children paint the shapes. Then add a coating of polyurethane or shellac to strengthen the figures.
7. Using craft glue, ask students to attach safety pins to the back of the dough, as shown, to complete the brooches.
8. Help the children wrap their brooches in tissue paper and tie closed with ribbons. Ask students to present the gifts to family members or friends on Valentine's Day.

Valentine Rhyme Time

1. Gather the class together in a circle.

2. Tell students that they are going to play a rhyming game. Begin the game by saying a word that has many rhymes (such as "tree," "far," or "so").

3. Ask the child sitting on your left to name a word that rhymes with that word. Continue around the circle, with each child trying to think of another word that rhymes. Write down the words on a chalkboard.

4. Encourage students to help their classmates when necessary. Continue playing until everyone is satisfied with the number of rhyming words that have been named. Then suggest another word and pick up the game at the point in the circle where it had stopped.

5. After a number of rhyming word lists have been created, ask children to try to think up valentine's poems using some of the words on the chalkboard.

Valentine Story Starters

1. Ask the children to make up stories about the silliest Valentine's Day ever. Give students suggested story starters to help them begin. Some possibilities are:

I opened the mailbox on Valentine's Day and saw...
The worst valentine I ever got was...
When I addressed the valentine to the wrong person...
I knew it was going to be a crazy Valentine's Day when I saw...
"Don't open that card!" my mother shouted.

2. Let students write or dictate their valentine stories. Encourage children to draw pictures to accompany their stories.
3. Staple the stories and illustrations on a Valentine's Day bulletin board. Title the bulletin board, "Silly Valentines."

Name _____

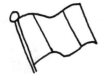 # Raise the Flag!

Canada's maple leaf flag was adopted on February 15, 1965. Match these flags to the names of their countries.

CANADA

GREAT BRITAIN

JAPAN

CHINA

SWITZERLAND

ISRAEL

SOUTH KOREA

UNITED STATES

NIGER

INDIA

Design and Discovery

National Inventor's Day is held on February 11 in honor of Thomas Edison, who was born on that day in 1847. Edison was interested in chemistry and other sciences at an early age. One of his first inventions was a stock ticker, and he used the money he received from selling this patent to set up his own laboratory in Menlo Park, New Jersey.

Perhaps Edison's most famous invention was the incandescent light bulb. He spent a great deal of time and money perfecting this invention. Edison also invented the phonograph, and he made improvements on the telegraph, the telephone, the camera, and many other things.

Thomas Edison received over 1,000 patents in his lifetime. Tell students that many children have received patents on their inventions. Ask each child to think of an invention. The invention may be something completely new and original, or it may be an improvement made to something that already exists.

Ask students to draw plans for their inventions. If possible, let children use available materials to make models of their inventions. Have a class "Inventors Fair," and invite other students and teachers to observe the inventions and how they work.

Encourage older children to research the patent procedure and explain how it works. Ask students to write patent applications for their inventions, describing what makes them unique and innovative.

Solar System Mobile

Mark the anniversary of the discovery of Pluto (February 18, 1930) by making this mobile with the class.

Materials:
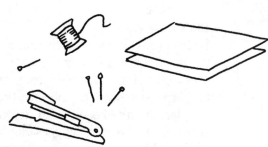
- different-sized Styrofoam balls
- crayons or markers
- construction paper
- straight pins
- stapler
- thread
- clothesline

Directions:

1. Divide the class into nine groups. Have each group research the properties of one of the planets (size, color, moons, rings, distance from the sun and earth, etc.).

2. Place different-sized Styrofoam balls in a pan. Tell each group to choose one of the balls to represent their planet. Help students select the balls that are in proportion to the size of their planets.

3. Tell each group to color their planet. Encourage each group to make any appropriate moons for its planet by cutting circles from construction paper. Then students may stick a pin through the center of the moon and into the Styrofoam planet, as shown. Some groups may also wish to make rings for the planets using construction paper that will fit snugly around the Styrofoam balls.

4. Use the largest size ball to represent the sun. Staple a piece of thread to the sun and tie it to the end of a clothesline, as shown.

5. When all the planets have been completed, have the class suspend them from the clothesline to show their respective distances from the sun. (Mercury is the closest, followed by Venus, Earth, Mars, Jupiter, Saturn, Uranus, Neptune, and Pluto.)

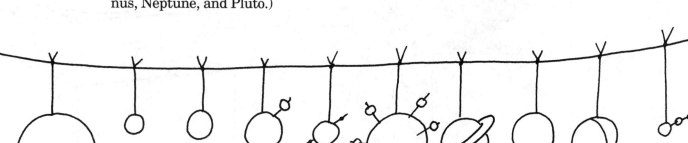

Silhouettes Bulletin Board

Celebrate George Washington's birthday on February 22 by making these silhouettes.

Directions:

1. Display coins so that the class may see whose profiles are on which coins.

2. Ask if anyone can explain what a profile is. Tell the class they will be making coin profiles using their own profiles.

3. Have each student choose either a silver or copper coin for his or her profile. Then tell each child to make a 10" diameter pattern of a circle to trace onto silver- or copper-colored construction paper and cut it out.

4. Tape black paper to a wall to make the profiles. Seat each child sideways in front of the wall and shine a film projector light on the child's profile. The shadow will appear on the paper, as shown.

5. Remind each student to keep his or her head still while the profile is being traced with white crayon or pencil.

6. Have each child cut out the profile, glue it to the coin background, and write his or her name on the back. Then have students use the pattern on page 93 to make coin profiles of George Washington.

7. Display students' profiles with the George Washington profiles on a bulletin board or a classroom wall. Ask the children to guess which profile belongs to which classmate.

Why the Bear Is Stumpy-Tailed

Many years ago, when the bear still had a tail, he met a fox who was carrying a large bundle of fish.

The bear's mouth watered as he admired the fox's catch. "However did you get so many fish in one day?" he asked the fox.

Now, the truth was that the fox had stolen the fish from a fisherman down the river. But the fox decided it would be fun to play a trick on the bear.

"It's really quite easy," said the fox. "All you need to do is carve a hole in the ice and stick your tail through. Then the fish will swim up to bite your tail and get stuck."

"This sounds like a good way to catch a big, tasty dinner," thought the bear. He thanked the fox and headed down to the river.

The bear carved the hole, then sat down on the freezing ice. His tail sank down into the icy water, chilling the bear even more. After a few minutes had passed, the bear still hadn't felt even a single tug.

"I'll wait just a little longer," the bear said to himself. "Surely I will have a yummy fish or two by then."

But of course, nothing happened. And by the time the bear decided he was too cold to stay out there any longer, the ice had frozen around his tail. He was trapped!

The poor bear pulled and pulled to try to free himself. Finally he gave one last great, big tug—and off came his tail.

Name _____

Why the Bear Is Stumpy-Tailed

1. What did the fox say when the bear asked him how he caught so many fish? _____

2. Why did the fox lie to the bear?_____

_____

3. Did the fox's method of catching fish work for the bear? _____

_____

4. Why did the bear keep sitting on the ice for so long? _____

_____

5. What do you think the bear learned from this experience?

_____

Answers

page 10

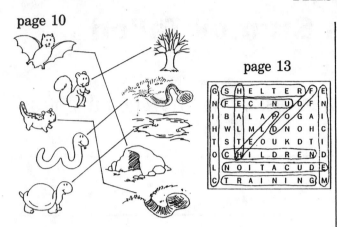

page 13

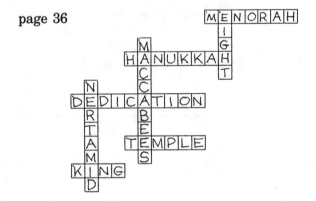

page 18

12 + 13 = 25	15 + 14 = 29	Goals scored:
7 + 9 = 16	19 + 22 = 41	285
21 + 8 = 29	10 + 14 = 24	
17 + 13 = 30	16 + 8 = 24	
32 + 12 = 44	1 + 22 = 23	

page 24
Answers may vary.

Possible unnecessary items:
bathing suit   beach ball
bicycle

page 36

```
            M E N O R A H
            |       |
            M       G
  H A N U K K A H   H
            C       T
    N       C
  D E D I C A T I O N
    E       B
    R       E
    T E M P L E
    A       S
  K I N G
    D
```

page 57
Answers may vary.

page 72

1. John F. Kennedy—1961-63
2. Thomas Jefferson—1801-09
3. Ronald Reagan—1981-89
4. George Washington—1789-97
5. Franklin D. Roosevelt—1933-45
6. Theodore Roosevelt—1901-09
7. John Adams—1797-1801
8. Abraham Lincoln—1861-65
9. Dwight D. Eisenhower—1953-61
10. Jimmy Carter—1977-81

page 74
Dear Deb,
   Feed the dog before bed.
                   Dad

page 80

msug—gums   vycita—cavity
rfeiould—flouride   ngllfii—filling
hubttrohso—toothbrush   srmloa—molars
ofssl—floss   ebti—bite
esttthaopo—toothpaste   tndiset—dentist

page 83
Answers may vary.
slavery—when a person is held in bondage by another person, institution, or government.
abolish—to do away with something so that it will never happen again.
secede—to formally leave or withdraw from an alliance, organization, or union.
emancipate—to free from bondage or slavery.

page 89

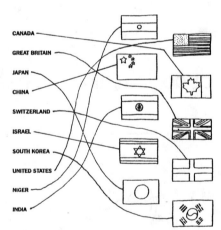

page 95
Answers may vary.
1. The fox said he carved a hole in the ice, stuck his tail through, and the fish bit his tail and got stuck.
2. Because the fox thought it would be fun to trick the bear.
3. No—his tail got stuck.
4. Because the bear was hungry and wanted a nice dinner.
5. The bear learned not to trust a fox carrying an armful of fish!